BIRTH OF AN ACTIVIST:
THE SOX KITASHIMA STORY

by
Tsuyako (Sox) Kitashima
and
Joy K. Morimoto

Published by:
Asian American Curriculum Project, Inc.
P.O. Box 1587
San Mateo, CA 94401
http://www.AsianAmericanBooks.com

Joy K. Morimoto and Tsuyako (Sox) Kitashima
Birth of an Activist: The Sox Kitashima Story/Joy K. Morimoto
ISBN: 0-934609-12-8 (pbk.):$19.95
Publication information on file.

Cover photo: Ted Kurihara Photo, San Francisco
Book design: Libby Oda (Petite Elf), San Francisco

⊕ ⊂⊃ 147 INKWORKS

for Aaron,
so that he may learn the value of friendship,
the importance of helping others,
and to fight for what he believes.

Be ashamed to die until you have won some victory for humanity.

HORACE MANN

Injustice anywhere is a threat to justice everywhere.

DR. MARTIN LUTHER KING, JR.

TABLE OF CONTENTS

ACKNOWLEDGEMENTS

This publication would not have been possible without the support and encouragement of many people. First and foremost, I am very grateful for the California Civil Liberties Public Education Program (CCLPEP) for funding this project. I thank the CCLPEP Board of Directors and staff for their exceptional leadership and service.

Birth of an Activist accorded me the wonderful opportunity to work closely with several of my dear friends and role models: my heartfelt "aloha" to Sox, for inviting me into her life to help tell her story; Diane Yen-Mei Wong, editor and advisor extraordinaire who provided invaluable guidance and expertise; and Carole Hayashino, for teaching me more than she will ever realize.

Thank you to Libby Oda for lending her abundance of talent to the cover and design of this book; Lewis Kawahara, my buddy since our graduate school years at UCLA and fellow CCLPEP recipient for his assistance and encouragement; Mei Nakano for initially leading me through the publishing maze; Rol Risska for his diligent proofreading; Kay Ochi for important leads and contacts; Alan Nishio for serving on my advisory committee; Jill Mari Shiraki for generously sharing helpful information; Ted Kurihara for his keen "eye" in photographing Sox for the cover; Susan Snyder of The Bancroft Library for her research assistance; and Florence Hongo and the Asian American Curriculum Project for offering such meaningful and generous support.

I extend my deep appreciation to Dale Minami, Carole Hayashino, and Bob Bratt for sharing their reflections on Sox, and to Sen. Barbara Boxer, House Democratic Leader Nancy Pelosi, and the Honorable Norman Y. Mineta for graciously contributing their comments.

After many years of work on this book, I thank my family and friends in Hawai`i, California, New York, and Indiana, for their constant encouragement. Above all, I thank my life partner Bruce for his unwavering support, and for never letting me stop believing this book was possible. We are thankful and delighted that our son Scott will grow up knowing real life heroes like Sox.

FOREWORD

I first met Sox Kitashima in the late 1970s, in my early years in the United States Congress. At the time, she was working on a proposal to give federal retirement credit to Japanese American federal employees who spent time in the U.S. Government's internment camps during the Second World War.

Like most efforts to which Sox has turned her hand over the years, she was successful.

There is no one in the Japanese American community who does not owe her a tremendous debt of gratitude for her advocacy on our behalf. Her drive, her energy, her persistence and her dedication have won some tremendous victories for us, and for the Nation.

Our incarceration at the hands of our own government during World War II has been called the greatest mass abrogation of civil liberties in our Nation's history. It was a betrayal of the United States Constitution's guarantees of due process and equal justice under the law.

At the same time, the story of the drive to redress that wrong is one of the redemption of our national honor, and a national rededication to our highest principles.

If there is any lesson to be drawn from the internment and the successful effort to secure redress, it is that our Constitution is only as strong as the will and the dedication of the American people. It is only as strong as our individual devotion to defending its ideals, and working to put them into practice.

If we had a Nation of Sox Kitashimas, I would have no fear for our future. As it is, I'm glad she's around to keep us on our toes.

The Hon. Norman Y. Mineta

Introduction

It was back in 1989 that I first met Tsuyako "Sox" Kitashima. During my stint as a staff writer with *Asian Week* newspaper, an English language weekly based in San Francisco, I was given the assignment of interviewing various Japanese Americans about issues of concern in the post-redress and reparations era. New to the Bay Area, I asked my colleagues for names of people to interview. One of them immediately said, "Be sure to call Sox."

An interesting name, I thought to myself. Curiosity got the best of me and I called Sox. Her warmth and enthusiasm quickly eased any anxiety I had felt, and she opened up to me as if I were an old friend. She was honest and forthright. The very next afternoon I had the pleasure of putting her voice to a face. What struck me immediately upon meeting Sox, as I'm sure most people would agree, was her brilliant silvery-white hair. She bounded over to me with hand outstretched and offered such a radiant and easy smile. I remember being thoroughly impressed then with her energy and youthful vigor. I still am.

From there we cultivated a friendship, meeting every week or two to have lunch and simply talk. Through Sox's eyes I was offered a glimpse into the trauma of the evacuation and internment, gained insight into the soul of the San Francisco Japanese American community, and witnessed the day-to-day struggle for redress and reparations, a cause that consumed her daily life. My admiration for Sox's integrity and strength of character came easily. She has absolutely no facades. What you see is really what you get.

When I later began working for the Japanese American Citizens League (JACL), a national civil rights organization headquartered in San Francisco's Japantown, I called upon Sox countless times for assistance. She never once refused a request to speak at a school or with the media about her wartime experience. And the requests were endless. The handful of former internees who were willing to speak publicly about their experiences seemed to grow smaller each month as more passed away or became ill. But you could always depend on Sox. She became the point person for redress in San Francisco because of her daily contact with the Office of Redress Administration in Washington, D.C. All of those daily long-distance calls, I should add, were made at her own expense. It was also Sox who, whenever called upon, traveled to Sacramento to testify before various state legislative committees on issues related to redress.

The local and national attention Sox has garnered — from the media, the federal government, community organizations, public officials, and others — is well deserved. Sox is a role model for us all, exemplifying the power of one person to impact the lives of so many for the better. She is an extraordinarily ordinary woman graced with enormous compassion and generosity. Her transformation into a grass-roots community activist has been nothing short of inspirational. I know I am not alone in considering myself blessed to know her in my lifetime.

The following story is told "from my heart," as Sox is fond of saying. I can only hope I have done her story justice.

I

The Simple Life

I was born Tsuyako Kataoka on July 14, 1918, in Hayward, California. People are always curious about how I came to be known as "Sox." Well, the "Tsu" part of my name, Tsuyako, was somehow very difficult for my non-Japanese friends to pronounce. They would stumble over it and mispronounce it time and again, calling me "Socko" and other variations, until they finally shortened it to "Sox." That nickname just stuck with me.

I've spent most of my life — except the years during World War II – in Northern California. I was born and reared in a town called Centerville, which was one of the districts of what is today known as the city of Fremont. Centerville was one of about eight small towns which comprised an area known as Washington township. If you blinked twice while driving through Centerville, you missed the whole town. But I suppose that was true of most of the towns in our area.

I come from a rather large family. There were six of us children. I'm the second youngest in my family as well as the youngest daughter. There was my father Masajiro, my mother Yumi, my three brothers Masao, Hisao ("Hiss"), and James ("Bo"), and my two older sisters Nobuko and Lillian. Both of my parents are deceased, as is Nobuko, who was the eldest, and my two older brothers, Masao and Hiss. My surviving siblings are Lillian (Hara), who lives in San Francisco, and the youngest of the Kataoka children, James, of Castro Valley, California.

My mother and father immigrated to America from Japan at the turn of the twentieth century. They were both from a prefecture in Japan called Yamaguchi, from a town called Yanai. My father's family home remains, and his nephew resides there today.

My mother was twenty-six years old when she came to America. A picture bride,[1] she arrived in the United States on the S.S. Korea, which left Yokohama, Japan, on April 4, 1905, and docked in San Francisco on April 20, 1905. My mother entered this country with fifty dollars to her name. For whatever reasons, port officials detained her right there at the dock.[2] I remember her stories about being confined near the water and not being allowed to enter the city to be with my father. She told us how disappointed she felt when she finally met our father face to face: because he had only sent pictures of himself taken from the waist up, she had expected a much taller man. That story always made us laugh.

Although I don't know the exact date of my father's entry into this country, I believe he came to San Francisco around 1902. He was thirty-six years old. Like most of the Issei, or first-generation Japanese immigrants to America, my parents came to this country full of hope and expectations. They sought good fortune and a better life than what they had had in Japan.

Unfortunately, there is much about my parents' childhood and youth that I know little or nothing about. Looking back, I wish that my siblings and I had taken the time to learn about their past or about Japan. I think one reason we never thought to ask them questions is because as Nisei, second-generation Japanese Americans, we didn't have any keen interest in Japan. After all, we were born in America and were Americans through and through. It is only now, perhaps, after the pain of World War II, that some of us Nisei are taking an active interest in learning more about the land of our ancestors.

After arriving in San Francisco, my father opened an American-style restaurant on Eddy and Fillmore streets. He wasn't fluent in English, and he didn't have any help from family members. He essentially ran the restaurant all by himself. His greatest asset had to be the fact that he was truly a talented cook. To this day the mouth-watering aroma and taste of his home-made hot rolls remain with me. My father made the best hot rolls I've ever had.

My mother didn't work in my father's restaurant, partly because she didn't know how to prepare American foods. The overriding reason, though, was she needed to help supplement the family income. The Kataokas were a growing family, and there were mouths to feed. So she found domestic work in San Francisco, cleaning and taking care of people's homes. Everyday before going to work, she would carefully wrap up a lone donut. That was her snack. Although my mother had difficulty learning the English language, she was able to get by with the basics. My father tried to help her out by writing down the words, "Hello," "Good-bye," "Thank you," and our address on a piece of paper, which she always kept with her. I guess he figured those were the most important things for her to know.

My parents' lives changed dramatically in April, 1906, when the devastating earthquake struck San Francisco. Fortunately they weren't hurt, but the trembler completely destroyed my father's restaurant. Immediately afterwards, my parents were among the hordes of people in the city who were fed and tended to by Red Cross volunteers.

After the quake, my father, at my mother's insistence, decided to quit the restaurant business entirely and go into farming. He couldn't see a future in the restaurant business. There was another reason for his decision, however. My siblings and I later learned that my father, as a business owner, had became a target of extortionists. I personally think it was because he was Japanese. A group of non-Japanese men approached him one day at his restaurant and tried to sell him "protection," as they called it.

They threatened him, saying that if he refused, he could expect trouble. These same men returned soon after and tried to break into the restaurant. My father happened to open the door and, as a result, got beaten up. That was the last straw. He wanted nothing more to do with them or the restaurant.

So farming became my parents' livelihood. Many of their Japanese friends also ventured into farming after the earthquake. Because the Issei could not become naturalized American citizens in those days, however, people like my parents were barred from purchasing any land.[3] My father leased some land in Niles, which was across the bay and down south from San Francisco. With the help of a friend he built a four bedroom house for our family. We later moved to Centerville, a farming area about three and a half miles away. We quite literally took the house with us: it was cut in half and towed in sections to Centerville.

My parents were involved in truck farming in various areas of Northern California: Hayward, San Juan, Centerville, Niles, and back to Centerville. Strawberries were their main crop, but they raised other produce as well, such as celery, lettuce, tomatoes, and cauliflower. When my siblings and I were old enough, we helped out. Even with all of us lending a hand, though, my parents often had to hire extra workers, especially during strawberry season. It was critical to harvest the crop early in order to get the best price for it.

While my parents never got rich off the land, farming provided our family with food and other basic necessities. It was a very hard life filled with long days and strenuous work. Most of the farmers in our area simply survived from year to year. Farmers harvested their crops with hopes of making some money, but whatever they made had to be immediately plunked into the next year's crop. I know my parents had their lean years trying to make ends meet, but thankfully, we didn't lack for food. All things considered, my father provided well for us, and we never expected luxuries anyway.

My mother was a good-natured, rather traditional person, who had a side to her that loved to instigate pranks and engage others in games. I remember she once played a game with a fellow named Yasuto Kato during a get-together at our house. She took a raw, unbroken egg and placed Yasuto's cap on the floor. She somehow convinced him to try and catch the egg as she passed it through the small opening between the door hinge and the wall. They did this back and forth, making everyone laugh with their animated gestures. Thank goodness Yasuto was quick, or else the egg would've broken right into his hat.

My mother was usually very cheerful and jolly and often sang to us kids, drumming her hands on whatever was around to keep rhythm. Even though farming was back-breaking, dirty work, you could always tell when my mother was out working because she sang as she pulled weeds or picked strawberries. She had a beautiful singing voice. Despite suffering from rheumatism in her knee, she hid her pain from others and toiled on the farm everyday. She also managed to care for six children.

My father also worked hard everyday of his life. He had a few unusual habits and idiosyncrasies worth mentioning. One was that he never went anywhere without wearing a necktie, not fancy silk ties or anything, but a tie nonetheless. He even wore a tie while he worked! People always commented on that. Imagine someone toiling behind a horse and plow wearing a necktie. My father used to say that he didn't feel completely dressed without a tie. He was also a very neat and tidy person, which was the opposite of my mother. The old saying that opposites attract proved true in our family.

Even though my family wasn't particularly religious — we were Buddhist — my father would say a prayer every night before going to bed. I often wondered what he prayed about. I don't think my mother ever prayed. But my father, no matter what hour of the night he came home, always made it a point to pray.

My father also had a unusual habit of saving every *umeboshi* (Japanese plum) seed he came upon. If he spotted a single seed on the ground, he would pick it up, wash it, and put it in a can. He'd get angry if he caught me or my siblings throwing away a plum seed. *Umeboshi* was somehow a sacred thing to him. He used to say that the seeds would make one's children intelligent. I guess he was disappointed because despite his abundant collection of seeds, there were no scholars in our family.

When I came of age, I attended Centerville Grammar School, a small school of a couple hundred students, ranging in age from kindergarten through eighth grade. Our school had a mixture of white and Japanese American students, as well as a few black students. We all got along as friends and schoolmates.

I was an average student. I enjoyed school, but I was no honor student. My favorite subjects were English and spelling. In my day teachers emphasized proper pronunciation and good penmanship, and they firmly believed in strictness and discipline. Back then, we all feared the school principal. We often heard him in the hallway, taking a yardstick to a "bad" student.

I have fond memories of my grammar school and some of the teachers. My first grade teacher in particular, Miss Mary Dias, left a lasting impression on many of us Nisei. Genuinely warm and dedicated, she treated everyone equally and fairly and made us feel special. Parents liked her too. During the strawberry season my father made sure she got baskets of fruit; it was my parents way of showing their gratitude for her kindness. Most of the teachers in our school were pleasant and nice, but I think Miss Dias went out of her way to make every student feel welcomed.

Though decades have passed, I can still picture my grammar school classroom. We had old fashioned windows, the ones you had push out to open and kept open with a pull of a chain. We had matching desks and chairs made out of clean, solid wood. Our desks had sturdy tops that lifted up, and we kept our books and papers inside. Each desktop also had a built-in inkwell. My girlfriends and I often picked flowers and put them in our inkwells, so that the ink would color and stain them. Some of the boys would make paper balls, dip them into the ink and, when the teacher wasn't looking, throw them at other students.

Recess period was the best time of the day. My friends and I loved playing all sorts of games like jacks, jump rope, hopscotch, and hide-go-seek. We especially liked a game called "Red Line." The object of the game was to pull opposing team members across a red line to your side, similar to tug-o-war. The boys usually got together among themselves and played marbles with great enthusiasm, vying for prized agates. We hated rainy days, though, because that meant we had to stay indoors in the school basement, which was a dark and cramped place.

The grammar school was filled with several bountiful almond trees. We Nisei students picked the trees clean of green almonds. Sometimes we'd bring salt from home wrapped in pieces of wax paper so that we could coat the almonds and eat them right away. Green almonds were a real treat. The trees didn't stand a chance against us.

Every afternoon after school, my brothers and sisters and I, along with many of our Nisei classmates, immediately headed off to Japanese language school. As charter members of the school, my parents wanted us to have an understanding and command of the Japanese language. In our family, though, my siblings and I really learned to speak Japanese from our parents, because they rarely spoke to us in English. Like most Issei, they spoke predominantly Japanese, with English words and phrases sprinkled in here and there.

As tiring as it was to attend language school in addition to our regular school, we had our share of fun at Japanese school, especially playing games and eating green apricots. Just as we raided the green almond trees at our grammar school, we'd pick green apricots straight off the tree in the schoolyard of the Japanese school, devouring them right then and there. They were sure tasty!

My formal Japanese language education didn't last very long and it shows. While I can converse rather fluently in Japanese today, I can neither read nor write it. We were living in Niles at the time, which was over three and a half miles away from the language school. The long distance made it difficult for my father to pick me and my brother Bo up everyday. Japanese school usually ended at 5 p.m., which meant that my father had to interrupt his work on the farm. So occasionally Bo and I walked home. We'd try to make a game of it, walking from one telephone pole to the next, then running, then kicking rocks, skipping, and doing all sorts of silly things to make the long walk seem shorter.

After Centerville Grammar School, I attended Washington Union High School, which had a fairly large student body of about five hundred students. By then we rode buses to school everyday. The thing about high school which stands out most in my mind was the immense popularity of athletic sports. People in the community and the surrounding areas attended many of our tennis, basketball, football, and baseball games. Many Nisei excelled in these sports, becoming stars in our eyes. Our school had an impressive gymnasium that Japanese American organizations frequently used for tournaments. I'd sometimes go and watch girls' and boys' basketball games in the evenings. That was my only opportunity to get out and socialize with other people my age.

Baseball was an especially popular pastime in the Japanese American community. During the baseball season, our entire family, strawberry season or not, attended all the games because my brothers played. My parents often traveled with the team to outlying areas. It was a big deal for all of us whenever our team won, because that meant someone's parents would treat everyone to a meal, most often a delicious Chinese dinner.

When I reflect on my younger days in Centerville, we had very little in the way of entertainment, and yet we found ways to have fun. Life was simple, and so we made a big deal about everything. Listening to the radio, for instance, became an important source of amusement for us at night. My sister and I would plant ourselves in front of the crystal set, sharing the earphones between us. Occasionally my brothers and sisters and I would sit around and play card games with the winner collecting Necco candy.

Dating wasn't very common among my group of friends. We found it difficult to go anywhere since teenagers rarely had their own cars. One car usually served the needs of the entire family, even a large family like mine. We had one movie house in our township, but you needed a car to get there. On rare special occasions, I would go to see movies in Oakland or San Jose with my friends.

Dances were quite popular in my generation. Community groups or area clubs usually sponsored the events, in which the music was provided by rented jukeboxes. Young Japanese Americans from as far away as San Jose, San Leandro and Hayward would come to our town for these dances.

Since I usually had to help out on our farm after school, I didn't attend many school dances or stay to watch games. Work on the farm always came first. I have to admit that I looked forward to rainy days because that meant I could stay inside the house. When I found myself with free time, I often went with my friends to the Centerville Library. The library was tiny, but we spent many hours there reading good books rather than doing our homework.

In retrospect, I learned a lot living on a farm and experienced things I wouldn't have in the city. Everyone in my family was expected to pitch in and help whenever and wherever help was needed. For example, I learned to drive a large, longbed truck that we used on the farm. I got around in it just fine, despite being as short as I am. Whenever our family sedan broke down, I'd hop in the truck and drive into town to do our shopping or run other errands.

I learned about manual labor and the value of money early on. Every year my sister Lillian and I earned extra money by harvesting apricots on a nearby ranch. Even the men folk, like my brothers, did similar work on the side, picking cherries and apricots. They'd make about thirty-five cents an hour, considered decent wages back then.

Lillian and I proved to be an efficient team. Our job was to cut and halve the apricots with a paring knife and carve out the pits. We'd set aside the pits in a coffee can, because like the fruit itself, they were sellable. We'd then lay out the apricot halves on a large tray that was sent on to the smokehouse. We made anywhere from eight to twelve cents for a huge tomato lug box full of apricots. If the apricots were large, we got eight cents for them, but if they were small, which was more desirable, we were paid a little more. It seemed no matter how hard we worked, though, we never made more than two dollars and fifty cents to two dollars and eighty cents a day — combined. We used the money we earned to buy our school clothes in the fall.

Lillian and I were pretty resourceful, and when we put our heads together we did things that surprised people who knew us. When work became especially hectic on the farm, for example, it was difficult for the men to find time to till the soil. Figuring we could help, Lillian and I would get behind the horse and plow. We were both short and petite, however, so neither of us could manage both the plow and the horse reins, as one person would normally do. So we improvised: she held one and I the other. We worked the fields that way. Each time a car approached on the nearby road we would abruptly stop what we were doing because we didn't want anyone to see how ridiculous we looked. We laughed a lot at ourselves. I think my father and family appreciated the fact that we showed initiative.

The other thing we got involved in, which friends thought was unusual, was *kendo* (Japanese fencing). Two of my brothers were also involved in *kendo*. I don't know if people were surprised because of our size or because we were female. Maybe it was a little of both. Although neither Lillian nor I entered any major tournaments, we did participate in local contests. We even once had to compete against each other. My sister knocked me over on the very first move by poking me in the throat. That quickly ended my *kendo* career. I guess we took up *kendo* for both the discipline it taught us and to satisfy my father. He was such a *kendo* enthusiast.

After I graduated from Washington Union High School in 1936, I continued to help out on our farm. I think most of us country girls were raised to believe that we had to do our part by staying at home and helping our families. It was expected of us. It seemed unusual back then for young people to leave home, so few of my friends went on to college. I never thought to leave home and strike out on my own because I believed my duty was to remain with my family.

During the off-season on our farm, I did domestic work to earn a little extra money. Most of what I made I contributed to the family household, sometimes buying meat or food for a night's dinner. I eventually found more satisfying work with a local Centerville doctor, whose nurse had recently gotten married and quit. At first I started out taking dictation but gradually took on more responsibilities. I learned to sterilize equipment and assisted the doctor with patients, even learning to administer shots to a diabetic man. I worried about that in particular, because I was just a country girl, the daughter of a farmer, but having these new responsibilities gave me a sense of pride and self confidence. The job turned out to be short-lived because of the outbreak of the war, but I enjoyed the work while it lasted. I know it was this early exposure which made my work in later years at a veteran's hospital such a fond experience. Had it not been for World War II and the evacuation, I believe I would've pursued a career in nursing.

Living in a small town like Centerville instilled in me a strong sense of community. People knew and helped one another, especially within the Japanese American community. And because our family was actively involved in the community, our home often served as a gathering place.

Although we were Buddhist, my family participated in the nearby Alameda Buddhist Temple only on special occasions, such as *obon*,[4] when my sisters and I would go to the temple for *bon odori* practices.[5] After learning the steps and movements to the various dances, we'd then teach them to people in our community. Sometimes the reverend would come to Centerville, accompanied by several Sunday school teachers, to conduct Buddhist services, called *katei shukai* (practice and fellowship). Several Japanese American families in my hometown had homes large enough to accommodate these services, and the community would be invited. The host family fed the reverend and the teachers. A few of these services were held at our house.

We entertained a lot in our house, especially during the rainy winter months when there wasn't much else to do. My father would make his wonderful hot rolls for my brother's friends, who'd often come to play pinochle at our home. Being a terrific and creative cook, my father developed quite a good reputation and was often asked to prepare food for special occasions in our community. One of his specialties was his *sashimi* (raw fish) preparation. He would skin the fish, slice its meat, put the slices back into the fish and cover it up again with its skin. At first glance the fish would appear as though it had never been touched.

Our annual community-wide events, which bring back many happy memories, provided us with fun and fellowship.

Every year the Washington township chapter of the Japanese American Citizens League (JACL), an organization involved in civic and social activities, staged an amateur talent show which featured singing, dancing and *shibai* (a show or dramatic performance). People enjoyed these shows and didn't hesitate to participate. My family got involved every year. The performers often met at our house to practice, and we'd end up laughing hysterically at the miscues and antics that went on. We always worried about whether the performances would go smoothly, but on the night of the show, things would usually go off without a hitch.

My siblings and I were somewhat musically inclined, so we performed in the amateur shows. None of us ever took formal music lessons. We just loved playing music together and pretended we were a band. I played the piano, accompanied by my brothers on the snare drum, saxophone, and banjo. Hiss was exceptionally talented and had a personality that made him popular and the life of the group. He played the clarinet in the high school band, but also taught himself to play the saxophone and the *shamisen* (a Japanese stringed instrument). The *shamisen* is made for right-handers, but Hiss, being a lefty, decided to restring it in order to play it correctly. He was clever in that way. I suppose our family "band" sounded decent enough, because we were once invited to perform at the Buddhist temple for *hanamatsuri* (a festival in celebration of Buddha's birthday). We were very excited and enthusiastic about our "gig."

Our community was annually treated to a Japanese movie screening, compliments of a Japanese grocer in our hometown who rented out the town hall. Everyone received actual invitations to this event. The grocer did this as a way of showing his appreciation to all of us for patronizing his store. It was a special event; I once even got a new dress for the occasion.

The other big annual event was the township community picnic. This usually took place in Centerville because there weren't too many places around that could accommodate a crowd of our size. The picnic site was literally in a cow pasture, so you had to be very careful where you walked and laid your blankets. Families packed their favorite lunches and snacks and picnicked with other families. For our family that meant bringing foods like rice balls with *umeboshi* (Japanese plum inside), *teriyaki* chicken (chicken seasoned with soy sauce, rice wine and other ingredients), *nishime* (Japanese-style stew) and *tsukemono* (pickled vegetables). People often came to the picnic to show off their new cars. We had organized games and a number of races — potato sack, spoon-and-egg, three-legged—with winners receiving coveted pencils, writing tablets, and crayons.

I was an active member in our local JACL, which had a membership of about fifty people. I got involved in the production of *The Coordinator*, which was our chapter's newsletter. We worked on this over at the Japanese language school. Every New Year's we published a special, home-delivered edition of *The Coordinator*. I took this project seriously and often worked into the wee hours of the morning, cutting stencils, typing, contributing club news, and trying to meet deadlines. I learned a great deal from the talented and dedicated staff we had. Toby Hirabayashi did much of the artistic work, while Vernon Ichisaka, the chapter president, did the editing and layout. I even got to write a column for the publication. While I tried my best to make it interesting and engaging, it lasted all of about two issues before the war broke out and changed our lives.

I attribute much of the constant activity in our home and our participation in the community to my father, who was a firm believer in community involvement. He constantly encouraged us, saying, "You can learn something by getting involved. To not do what you can is bad; you learn what is good by being with others who are doing good."

The holiday season was always my favorite time of the year. I have many wonderful memories, especially of Christmases. One year my brothers and sisters and I dressed my mother up as ol' St. Nick. We stuffed her clothes to the brim with several pillows, pasted a Santa's beard on her chin, and colored her face with heavy rouge. She was such a good sport.

After getting her all made up, we decided to drive to her friends' homes and surprise them. We'd ring their doorbells and then hide behind some bushes, leaving my mother standing at the door. Most of her friends were bewildered and shocked upon opening the door, unable to recognize her at first. It was hard to stifle our laughter and giggles. One of my mother's friends, Mrs. Ushijima, was thrilled by our visit and commented that a visit from Santa Claus was a good omen. She said she knew the coming year would be a very lucky one. She thanked us over and over and served us refreshments. That was a memorable Christmas for me.

As in most Japanese and Japanese American families, New Year's, or *oshogatsu*, was an important and busy time of the year for us. Every year four or five families would come to our home with anywhere from fifty to eighty pounds of rice each. We'd pound the rice into *mochi* (steamed rice pounded into a rice cake), which is a symbol of strength, long life, and good fortune. *Mochitsuki* (the making of mochi) lasted all day long.

In preparation for the *mochi* pounding, my father got up very early in the morning. Outside of our home he built a barbecue pit in which he'd start a roaring fire. We'd wash the uncooked grains of rice first to remove sediment and dirt. My father would then transfer the washed rice into wooden trays, which he had also made. He'd place the trays over the fire to steam the rice. Once the rice was cooked, it had to be quickly removed from the trays and placed in an *usu* (mortar), where it was repeatedly pounded with a wooden mallet. The result was *mochi*, a glutinous and hot mass of rice. The young men pounded and turned the *mochi*. Pounding required brute strength and synchronous timing between the pounder and the person handling the rice. The work is exhausting and dangerous because a person can be struck and seriously hurt by the mallet if his timing is off.

While the men worked outside, we worked feverishly inside to shape and fill the pounded rice with sweet brown beans. We had to work quickly because rice hardens very fast. It was messy work and everything and everyone in the kitchen ended up blanketed with white flour, as though a snowstorm had passed right through our kitchen. In addition to eating the *mochi* with earnest, some of our friends made round, oversized *mochi* to place in their homes as an offering for a peaceful new year, while others crafted tiny ones to place in the trunks of their cars to protect them from mishaps and accidents.

My mother proved a whirlwind of activity every New Year's as she rushed around preparing a hearty lunch for everyone. *Oshogatsu* was one of the cultural traditions my parents impressed upon my siblings and me. They always spoke of *mochitsuki* as a sacred time, and to this day it remains an important holiday in our family.

My father was a real stickler for following certain traditions. Just prior to the actual new year, for example, we couldn't sweep or clean the house. That was considered bad luck, as though you were sweeping away all the good spirits. He used to say, whatever you do on New Year's eve determines what you do for the rest of the year. Needless to say, we kept that foremost in mind as we went about our business that day. We also made sure to bathe on the eve, in order to be clean as we greeted in the new year. All of us in my family grew up accepting these beliefs as a way of life.

The beginning of any new year signaled an especially hectic time for me. That's because my father believed we had to put up new wallpaper in our house each new year. Another one of his unique traditions. After my two older sisters married and moved out of the house, I did this job by myself. It was no easy feat, and even became comical at times. I managed to find ways to compensate for my shortness, like using a broomstick to push the wallpaper up into the corners. Sometimes the glue wouldn't stick and the wallpaper would peel away and come tumbling down on top of me. What a sticky, gooey mess!

In 1938 tragedy struck when my father was diagnosed with cancer of the esophagus. By then, my father had partially retired and spent a good deal of time working on a fish pond in our yard. Hiss had taken over much of the work on the farm.

My mother broke the news to my father. She felt terrible about telling him the prognosis, but she had to because she felt it wasn't fair to him not to know. The news obviously upset my father a great deal. Our doctor, a local Japanese man, had instructed my mother to start giving my father only very soft or liquefied foods. After that, we prepared separate meals for ourselves and for him. We all felt bad when we ate things that my father couldn't, such as meats.

The one thing we were thankful for, though, was that my father didn't experience any pain. At least we thought he wasn't, because he never complained. Certainly if my father had been in constant pain, it would've been very hard on my mother. The only physical sign of his illness was that he didn't eat enough and as a result was getting very thin. We resorted to boiling all sorts of herbs for him to drink.

Over the ensuing months, my father had an increasingly difficult time swallowing, eating, and speaking. The cancer worsened very quickly. We tried to ease his discomfort by giving him a bell to ring whenever he needed us. My mother and I did our best to tend to his needs, no matter the hour of the day or night.

Ironically, it was during my father's illness that I first spent time away from home. Friends of our family, the Norrises, invited me to accompany them on a week-long vacation to Long Beach, California, and help care for their son, whom I often babysat. The father, Alan Norris, was a judge in our town and rather prominent in the community. I had never been away from my family before for any extended period of time. I hesitated to leave given my father's condition, but my mother encouraged me to go, assuring me that everything would be all right. I worried throughout the entire trip.

One lighthearted moment during the trip came when the Mr. and Mrs. Norris asked me to make tapioca pudding for their son. I hadn't made anything like that before. I read the instructions but ended up making so much of it that we had enough to feed an army. They got a kick out of that.

I ended up sharing a double bed with the Norris' son, who was about a year old. During his naps, I often stared out the window at the beach below, watching families playing on the beach together, throwing a beach ball around and having the time of their lives. I felt very lonely. I guess it must've shown, because one day Mr. and Mrs. Norris asked if I had any friends in the area, which I did. An old friend of mine worked in a supermarket in Santa Monica, which was some ways away. They gave me a day off and put me on a bus to visit with him. But even that didn't ease my homesickness. I couldn't wait to get home. No matter how beautiful the restaurants we ate in or the places we visited, they didn't appeal to me at all at the time.

I was thrilled when the week finally passed and we headed home.

In the wee hours of the morning on December 6, 1940, my mother and I awoke to the sound of the ringing bell. My father asked to be moved into the rocking chair near the wood stove in the kitchen. He was cold, he said. We placed him in the chair and gently covered him with a blanket. He insisted that we go back to bed since it was still quite early. Later that morning one of my mother's friends came to visit, saying she wanted to see my father. Maybe something told this woman that my father wasn't going to live much longer. She tried talking to him but my father wouldn't or couldn't respond. He was nearly comatose. The woman turned to my mother and said, "I think something's happening to him.

Maybe you ought to call the doctor." So we called the doctor, and he told us that my father was in the "last stage." He administered a shot to my father to make him more comfortable. Soon after that my father died. He was seventy-two years old.

My father's friends arranged a beautiful funeral for him. In those days, Buddhist families were allowed to keep the body of their loved one at home overnight in order to hold a wake. One of my father's friends, with whom he often played *go* (a Japanese version of checkers) during the winter, sat beside the coffin and kept vigil throughout the entire night, urging the rest of us to go on to bed and get some rest.

Since coming to America my father hadn't once been back to Japan. As he grew weaker during his illness, he expressed a desire to return there, and so my mother wanted to honor his dying wish. On January 9, 1941, my mother and sister Nobuko set sail to Japan on the *Asama Maru* to take my father's ashes back to Yamaguchi prefecture. There they had a tombstone erected for him.

Disturbing rumors of war abounded while my mother and Nobuko were in Japan. Nobuko was bilingual in English and Japanese. Because of her skill, several Japanese newspapers approached her with job offers of one kind or another. She declined them all. Had she and my mother stayed on longer in Japan, they might've been stranded there during the war. We were very thankful that they returned when they did.

My mother was a strong person. After my father died, she carried on her work on the farm. My mother didn't brood over anything for too long; she simply accepted what life dealt her. That was her way.

II

Broken Dreams, Shattered Lives

Italicized passages in this manuscript are comments or observations I have inserted to provide a historical social context for Sox's statements.

On the morning of December 7, 1941, my mother, my sister Lillian, and I were in our car when the shocking news came over the radio that the Japanese had bombed Pearl Harbor. My mother's reaction was immediate. "This is terrible!," she exclaimed in Japanese. Lillian and I were stunned, and I plainly remember wondering how we would now be treated since we looked like the enemy.

Our way of life changed. Dramatically. Literally overnight we had gone from being Americans to being the "enemy." Local authorities and FBI agents came to our home with a list of names of Japanese American community leaders inquiring as to their whereabouts. I was frightened and began worrying about what was going to happen to us. One by one, community leaders were swiftly apprehended and taken into custody with no explanation given to their families. These were ministers, school teachers, business people, and presidents of community organizations — loyal and patriotic people whom we felt the government had no reason to distrust.

Some of our non-Japanese friends avoided us. I don't think they wanted to be pegged 'Jap [*sic*] lovers.' Even our neighbors, to whom we used to give fruits from our farm, stopped coming around. While I hadn't really encountered hostility and prejudice in town up until then, I recall a few kids using the word

"Jap"[*sic*] around me. The only person I ever sensed racist feelings from was our local postmaster. An older man of Portuguese descent he'd always try to strike up a conversation with me. Back then, we'd go to the post office to pick up our mail from a locked mailbox. Whenever I went to pick up the mail, he'd quickly take our mail out of the box so that I'd have to retrieve it from him personally. After Pearl Harbor, he'd say to me, "So what do you think is going to happen to you people?" He made me feel very intimidated.

Perhaps because we lived so close to the main highway, the police seemed to check out our house often. In the evenings they would shine a spotlight into our kitchen window. We had no idea if they were merely trying to frighten us or whether they really suspected us of wrongdoing. On one of their visits, they apparently took note of a box of tin on our back porch. They returned the next day and noted that it was gone. They interrogated my mother, demanding to know if she was secretly sending metal to Japan. How ridiculous, we wanted to scream at them! My brother explained that he used the tin to patch a hole in his car muffler. After that, we covered our kitchen window with a blanket whenever we stayed up late, to block out the intrusive spotlights and deter police from knocking on our door.

Days and weeks went by; fear, confusion, and uncertainty grew. Rumors spread that anything from Japan or things Japanese would automatically make one or one's family a suspect. Like many other families, we started a bonfire in our backyard and burned remnants of our past: pictures of my parents' family and relatives, Japanese newspapers, books, calendars, address books — anything written in Japanese. In her haste, my mother accidentally burned her bankbook.

Government officials ordered us to turn in all radios and cameras to the local police station because these were deemed 'contrabands.'[6] Our local police, however, were ill prepared for this situation, and so we received no receipt for our valuable possessions.

President Franklin D. Roosevelt, on February 19, 1942, signed Executive Order 9066, which authorized the establishment of military areas and the exclusion of any and all persons from these areas. The order set into motion the mass removal and incarceration of persons of Japanese ancestry from the West Coast. Even though the Executive Order never explicitly used the words "Japanese" and "Japanese Americans," only those persons of Japanese ancestry were affected. Italian and German Americans were not rounded up en masse, even though America was also at war with Italy and Germany. General John C. DeWitt, military commander of the Western Defense Command, issued formal notices excluding civilians from these restricted areas. He specifically ordered the evacuation of all Japanese persons,[7] both alien and nonalien, by a certain time on a prescribed date.

The removal of Japanese from the western coast of the United States began as early as March, 1942; in the San Francisco area, evacuation and detention began in April, 1942.

Until I actually saw evacuation notices posted on telephone poles and in other public places, it had never entered my mind that we would, or could, ever be physically removed from our homes and community. In many instances individuals and families had as little as forty-eight hours notice to dispose of all their property and lifetime possessions.[8] I had somehow convinced myself that travel restrictions and curfews placed upon us would be as bad as things would get.

As a JACL member, I, along with several other members, assisted fellow Japanese Americans with some of the paperwork required by the government for the evacuation. We helped type up family history forms and inoculation cards. The family history form included information about one's medical history and any chronic conditions. We lugged around our typewriters with us wherever we were needed. We traveled to surrounding areas, such as Brentwood, an area over fifty miles east of Centerville, to assist Japanese Americans living there with these forms. Harry Konda, who was active in our community, took charge of this program. Yet even at this stage, it felt like an exercise, and I had difficulty believing we would really be forcibly removed from our homes. We were Americans.

Our local high school, Washington Union, decided to hold a special graduation ceremony prior to the evacuation for the few Japanese American students. JACL president Vernon Ichisaka and I attended this event as chapter representatives. Vernon was well regarded by people in our community, such as our school principal, because he had excelled scholastically while in school. He gave a very emotional speech about patriotism and noted his deep appreciation for the ceremony. He did a wonderful job and would've moved anyone to tears. The school's gesture touched me, especially when some of my former teachers came over to hug me, saying how sorry they were that we were being taken away. I cried through most of the ceremony.

The owner of our local dime store also sympathized with us. An older Caucasian woman, she said to me that she was sorry to see us go. Her Japanese American customers had been "good customers" and people she could trust.

Faced with the impending evacuation, we often found ourselves in a dilemma, confused and anxious, as we tried to follow conflicting governmental orders. For example, Japanese Americans couldn't travel over five miles without a special permit, yet we had to travel over five miles to obtain the permit in the first place.

The government notices instructed us that we could take with us only what we could carry with both hands. That meant two suitcases per person. Back then, travel was considered a luxury, and so many people didn't own luggage. Folks in our community had to drive to a larger town just to find decent suitcases. Greedy and heartless merchants "jacked up" prices for the items we needed, but we had no choice.

My sister Nobuko and her husband Tom Fukuoka returned home to live with us prior to the evacuation, so that we would be together as a family. Nobuko no longer worked on our farm, but instead worked as domestic help for our landlord's family. She did everything for them, from chopping wood and cooking all the meals, to sewing their clothes and caring for their children. She could do it all, and she was an extremely hard worker. Our landlord was lost without her. When Nobuko and Tom came to live with us, Nobuko carried with her their life savings and the money from the sale of their home in Alameda. She placed all of this money in a coffee can and buried it in our backyard until our departure, which was a few days away. Unfortunately, it rained and water managed to seep into the can. When Nobuko unearthed the can, she found the bills badly crinkled, and so she patiently ironed each one. We didn't know whether to laugh or cry when we saw her doing this.

My sister Lillian, her husband Frank Hara, and their daughter Connie, who was about two-and-a-half years old, lived in the neighboring town of Newark. They would also evacuate with us.

As was the case with most other Japanese American families, non-Japanese came to our house looking to buy for a pittance whatever we couldn't possibly take with us. They knew they had us over a barrel, especially when some of them came only a few days before our departure. We resigned ourselves to accept whatever people offered or else leave things to be stolen. Hiss sold his two vehicles, a truck and his prized Caterpillar tractor, for cheap. Some individuals sold their brand new cars for a mere one hundred dollars.

We had great difficulty parting with some of our possessions. We owned an old horse that we used to work the farm. Since we didn't have a tractor to plow the fields, this horse had proved invaluable. My mother worried about its welfare. She kept reminding my brothers to "do something about the horse." While we were able to sell the car, truck, and other farm equipment without too much trouble, the horse, being as old as it was, was of little value to anyone. No one wanted it, and we couldn't even give it away. My brother finally found someone to take the horse. The buyer was going to have it destroyed. We all cried as the man led the horse away.

We had a pet dog, too, that we had raised since he was a puppy. We treated him like a human when he was little, hand feeding him with a bottle, using a balloon as a nipple. Just before the evacuation he ran out onto the highway chasing after another animal. A car hit him and injured his leg, which became infected. I took him to a veterinarian in Hayward, and to my horror the doctor suggested putting him to sleep at once. I didn't know what to do. Frantic, I telephoned Nobuko. We made a hard and traumatic decision that the more humane thing was to put our dog to sleep rather than let him suffer. We sobbed over the phone. My family felt very attached to this dog but we wouldn't have been allowed to take him with us. It was one of the most painful things I've ever had to do, and because of that, I've never wanted to have another pet.

Of the few material possessions we owned, parting with my piano was probably the hardest. My father had scrimped and saved to buy it. I loved playing the piano and it provided a good diversion for all of us. I suppose we were somewhat relieved when someone finally came and bought it, because we would've hated to leave it behind. I not only gave the buyer all of my sheet music, but in frustration, I also tossed in my tennis racket and whatever else I had that I knew I couldn't sell in time.

Our neighbor and landlord Mrs. Evelyn Stevenson Perkins had always been friendly to our family. She was a pioneer rancher who married a Perkins (of Jackson Perkins rose fame). A tall and slender woman so full of energy, she was physically strong but also very soft-hearted. She was probably one of the few people around town who wasn't afraid of being called a 'Jap [sic] lover.' On the morning of our departure, May 9, 1942, Mrs. Perkins invited our whole family over for breakfast. I offered to help serve, since there were so many of us, but she firmly said, "No, today is my day to serve you." She prepared a wonderful meal for us on her beautiful china. Her generosity and kindness really touched us. I found myself choking back tears as I ate. Mrs.

Perkins then drove us to the Japanese language schoolyard — one of the assembly sites — where we waited to board the buses that would take us away. She kept her composure as we said our good-byes. I think she tried to remain stoic for our sake.

The only other friendly non-Japanese face I saw that day was that of a young, Caucasian man who ran the local California Inn, a popular hamburger joint in our town. He stood outside of the schoolyard fence. He was younger than I, and a very likable and friendly guy. He had a slender build and walked with a limp, apparently caused by polio when he was a child. The inn had become a hangout for many Japanese Americans. My brothers used to go there with their friends and play the pinball machines, which were a rarity in Centerville. This young man came to see off some of his friends. That was the last time I ever saw him.

Our family followed the evacuation orders to a tee. Each of us carried two suitcases. Our family identification number, 21373, remains forever ingrained in my memory. These numbers were marked on everything we owned.

In my suitcases, which weren't very large at all, I packed only the most necessary and basic items. I didn't pack all of my clothes, because I didn't know whether they would be appropriate for wherever we were going. Neither did I buy any new clothes except for a pair of low cut, boot-style shoes lined with wool. I figured they would serve me well no matter where we went. Since we had to pack all of our toiletries — toothbrushes and toothpaste, creams, as well as linens — there wasn't much room for anything else. Little did I know then that I would live out of these two small suitcases for the next three years and four months.

The schoolyard was a scene of chaos and confusion. My memory of that day was seeing people with fear and anxiety in their eyes, rather than tears or sorrow. We didn't know what to going to happen to us.

The stigma I carried then as an 'enemy' weighed heavily. None of my non-Japanese friends came to see me off, and I thought to myself how quickly they had changed. As I stood in the schoolyard, a wave of loneliness and sadness swept over me. Those friends who never came to say good-bye only compounded the feeling of humiliation I felt. The coldness and the suspicion cast upon us by the government and our fellow Americans left me so dispirited and angry. How could my own country believe that I was the enemy when all that I had ever known was to be a patriotic American? The stigma stayed with me for a long time.

All of the propaganda at the time declared that we were being evacuated for "our own protection," when in actuality everything pointed to racial prejudice as the primary reason for our removal.[9] We were on our way to Tanforan racetrack. I cried the whole way.

III

HOME IS A HORSESTALL

The Tanforan horse racetrack in San Bruno, California, about fifteen miles south of San Francisco, was hastily converted into a temporary World War II detention camp [10] for Americans of Japanese ancestry from the San Francisco area. Tanforan opened on April 28, 1942, and closed on October 13 of that year. It was one of fifteen such camps scattered throughout California, Arizona, Oregon and Washington built to temporarily house Japanese Americans until the construction of more permanent ones. At its peak, Tanforan housed over eight thousand internees. [11]

The temporary detention camps, like their permanent successors, the internment camps, were nothing short of prisons, surrounded by barbed wire and armed guards. Confined within the barbed wire area, internees risked being shot if they tried to escape. A civilian branch of the U.S. Army, the War Relocation Authority (WRA), operated the camps.

Today, the racetrack and any physical remnants of the detention camp have vanished. A modern shopping center stands in their place.

I was twenty-three years old when I entered Tanforan.

Over two-thirds of the 120,000 people eventually interned were American citizens. The Issei, people like my parents, couldn't become naturalized American citizens because of laws enacted in this country that barred Asians from becoming citizens. They were deemed unassimilable. The Issei had no choice about citizenship and bore the status of "aliens." Those of us who were American citizens by birthright were called "non-aliens" by the government. Anyone with as little as one-sixteenth Japanese blood was interned. [12]

I was absolutely horrified when the military police physically searched me for contraband before entering Tanforan grounds. I didn't expect it at all. Everyone, young and old, was subjected to this hand search.

We had received advanced warning of things we couldn't bring: radios and cameras, liquor, scissors that were four inches in length or longer. Any item that could be used as a weapon — knives, straight razors — was confiscated. One of my girlfriends, however, managed to smuggle in a razor for her father so that he could shave. Prior to the evacuation we were instructed that only safety razors would be allowed in the centers. My girlfriend's father practiced with one but somehow couldn't get the hang of it. So my friend hid a straight razor in a box of feminine sanitary napkins. As two military policemen checked her suitcases, one of them asked her what was in the box that she had neatly wrapped in brown paper. He then realized they were sanitary napkins and said to the other MP, with embarrassment, "Oh, you know what that is." He didn't bother checking inside. She's lucky she got away with it.

I'll never forget my first meal at Tanforan. It consisted of discolored cold cuts, overcooked Swiss chard, and moldy bread. I refused to eat and wept openly. The humiliation was simply too much for me to handle, but the worst was yet to come.

Shock set in as I realized that this track and its horsestalls were to be my new "home." Until then, I had no idea what a racehorse track even looked like.

There were no steps in front of the horsestalls assigned to my family, number 21373. A swinging half-door divided our twenty-by-nine-foot stall from the next. As we stepped inside, the sight of horse manure laying on the floor and horse hairs stuck to the rough, whitewashed walls stunned us. There was no ceiling above us, just open space. We looked at each other and no one said a word. We felt numb. We put our belongings down and picked up the sacks we had been issued. We filled them with hay

42

from the pile outside the stall. These were our mattresses. I snuck a glance at my mother to see how she was coping. I waited for her to break down and cry over our awful surroundings, but she kept her composure. It was I who cried myself to sleep and said, "I can't believe I'm in America."

My mother, three adult brothers, and I shared one horsestall. James, mother and I shared the rear of the stall, while Masao and Hiss slept near the front. Nobuko and Lillian, their spouses, and my niece Connie, lived in the stall next to us. We couldn't clean our horsestalls because we had no buckets or containers in which to haul large amounts of water. And the stench of manure remained. We lived like that for the duration of our Tanforan stay.

The horse stables consisted of ten stalls on each side. With no ceilings or soundproof walls, you could hear everything: families arguing, babies crying, and the sick coughing throughout the night. There was no privacy whatsoever, with knotholes and peepholes in the walls for those who were nosy. People who had packed away items like Ajax cleanser used it to smear windows, providing some privacy. Given the limited amount of belongings we were allowed to bring with us, there was no room for luxuries like curtains.

On several occasions, our former landlord Mrs. Perkins visited us at Tanforan. The only place we could meet visitors was at the perimeter fence. She brought with her food and clothing.[13] She was even kind enough to offer to repair my broken wristwatch. Once she brought me a couple of cotton dresses, which first had to be examined by the guards. To me, even a stick of gum was something to be appreciated and so her gesture was overwhelming. We felt gratitude toward Mrs. Perkins for her friendship and generosity. To this day I often think about her. She was unafraid of what people said or thought about her association with Japanese Americans. She looked out for our family, especially where my mother was concerned.

On one visit, Mrs. Perkins had pulled up pieces of linoleum from the kitchen floor of our house in Centerville and brought

them to Tanforan. We used the pieces to try to block out the continual draft in the horsestall and prevent my mother's rheumatism
in her knee from worsening. Her knee was really bad — it had
swelled to the size of a football — so she couldn't walk to the mess
hall. My sister Nobuko brought my mother her meals everyday.

A canteen was set up where we could purchase toothpaste, tis-
sues, sanitary napkins, cigarettes, and other small items, but unless
you lined up early in the morning, these items sold out quickly. As
the weeks dragged on, people were allowed to buy goods through
mail order catalogs like Sears & Roebuck. At first we were cautious
and hesitant about doing this because we couldn't be sure that we'd
receive what we ordered and paid for. But given the lack of alternatives, we were glad we at least had this option.

Some people made attempts to lighten the mood around
camp. Sadie Towata, who was a pianist, and Goro Suzuki [14]
organized musical activities. Goro liked to sing and encouraged
other crooners to participate. Listening to the music sometimes
helped me to relax.

On one occasion I was able to leave Tanforan under guard for
a couple of hours to visit a Japanese American fellow at a sanitarium in Redwood City, a city not too far from the detention center. This man had been a houseboy for a Japanese American
businessman in our hometown. When the evacuation began, the
businessman's wife decided that she wanted the houseboy to evacuate with them. Sadly, while in Tanforan, the houseboy became
sick and was diagnosed with tuberculosis. He had to be isolated
from the rest of us, and so he was moved to a sanitarium. For
some reason, which I never understood, he put my name down
as a friend even though I didn't know him very well. One day
camp officials came to my horsestall, told me that this man wanted to see me, and drove me to Redwood City in a special military
police car. The man was gravely ill. It turned out that he really
didn't have anything in particular to tell me but just wanted to
talk. I think he was feeling lonely and didn't want to die alone.

I didn't look for work during our stay at Tanforan, partly because jobs were not plentiful. I filled my days with chores, such as trying to keep my mother and my three brothers in clean clothes. I'd get up early in the morning to do our family's wash. Hot water was in limited supply in the camps, which made it especially hard for mothers with babies and young children; they needed the water to wash their children's diapers.

Life at Tanforan remains the most grim period of my life. Absolutely nothing came easy for us. We had to walk several blocks to take our showers or to use the latrine, which was nothing more than a three-sided makeshift toilet with no door. Located on the way to the mess hall, it served hundreds of people. A shower was eventually built closer to our stable just prior to our leaving Tanforan. Like everything else in camp, private acts like showering and using the latrine always happened in the presence of others. A gentleman sacrificed a precious piece of his clothing, an undergarment, hanging it in such a way so that our face was shielded when we used the toilet. That person gave up a lot for the rest of us because we didn't have much clothing to begin with.

I realized that there were an awful lot of things I had taken for granted in life. Although we didn't have many amenities in Centerville, we had even less in Tanforan. I didn't appreciate what it meant to have a bathroom in the house until an incident occurred in Tanforan. It seems humorous in retrospect although it wasn't at the time.

Early one morning, while it was still very dark, I awoke and had to go to the bathroom. I was having a miserable bout with diarrhea and urgently needed to relieve myself. With the military police positioned directly above our stable, though, I feared being shot if they thought I was trying to escape. It even crossed my mind that the person who shot me would probably be considered a hero. With those thoughts utmost in my mind, and given the fact that the toilet was blocks away, I desperately scrounged

around our stable and was lucky enough to stumble upon a coffee can. It was a godsend.

Sanitation was horrible and primitive in Tanforan. About
twenty-four toilets served the entire population. In some camps
a long wooden plank with holes notched out of it served as toilets. Every twenty minutes or so a gush of water passed beneath
the plank to wash away the excretion. A person unfortunate
enough to sit on the first hole inevitably got soaked. The area
surrounding the communal toilets was always wet and sticky so
pieces of scrap lumber were laid down to use as stepping stones.
Some people, though, had it worse. Internees living below the
racetrack area dealt with raw sewage running directly in front of
their stables.

Day to day life in Tanforan took its toll on everyone, especially the Issei, who came with nothing to this country only to
have everything they worked so hard for taken away. We had no
control over our lives. Whoever was appointed to make our lives
miserable did an excellent job.

IV

WALLS OF DUST

The War Relocation Authority (WRA) administered the permanent camps that confined 120,000 Japanese Americans forcibly removed from the West Coast.[15] *Like its nine other counterparts, Topaz, Utah, was located in a dismal, isolated and forsaken area.*

After four dreary months at Tanforan, we packed up our belongings and endured another evacuation. We boarded trains this time. Tanforan was abuzz with talk that all of us would be sent inland and exterminated upon our arrival at Topaz, Utah. The rumors proved false, of course, but caused such stress and anxiety among us because we didn't know what lay in store for us.

We boarded an old and dirty train. The soldiers ordered us to keep the window shades drawn. They said it was to keep us safe from potential snipers. Enroute to Topaz I learned from a fellow passenger, who must've peeked under the shade, that we passed my hometown of Centerville. I don't know when we passed through, but maybe it's best that I didn't know because I would've been heartsick. The only time the soldiers let us lift up the shades was when we entered the Great Salt Lake in Utah; they probably thought no one would try to shoot us there.

It took nearly three days to reach our destination.[16] After arriving in Delta, a small farming town seventeen miles from Topaz, we boarded buses bound for Topaz.

As we approached the camp, I saw rows of tar-papered barracks, some not yet finished. Topaz looked like a desolate, barren, sagebrush-laden desert. Mountains surrounded the camp, but we were in the desert with dust swirling everywhere. [Topaz derived its name from the landmark Topaz Mountain, about nine miles northwest of the camp.] Internees who had arrived at Topaz before us wrote and forewarned us that we needed high-top boots because of all the scorpions and rattlesnakes in Utah. Men and women alike began ordering boots in earnest from the catalogs. We came dressed for the desert, resembling cowboys and cowgirls of the Old West.

We initially believed that Topaz was a resettlement community for Japanese Americans, a town where we would be free to do as we pleased. Reality told us otherwise. Like Tanforan, barbed wire fences surrounded us; military guards, some armed with machine guns, kept watch over us. The cry at Topaz, as in other camps, was "Don't go near the fence!" or else you risked being shot to death.

Compared to the cramped living quarters in the various detention centers, housing for internees in the permanent internment camps was somewhat larger but not by much. In Topaz, the twenty-by-one hundred and twenty ft. barracks were partitioned into six rooms. The larger of the rooms measured twenty-by-twenty-five-feet; the smaller rooms, sixteen-by-twenty-feet.

Our family lived in Block 16. Each block consisted of seventy-two rooms in twelve barracks and housed two hundred or more people. At its peak, over eight thousand internees (and about an additional two hundred Caucasian personnel) resided in Topaz, making it, ironically, the fifth largest city in Utah.[17]

Each block had a laundry room, a mess hall, toilets, and one communal bathtub. The toilets and bathtub had no doors, and the toilets themselves lacked seats. Shy women often waited until after midnight to take a bath. Only after rigorous protest by internees did camp officials erect partitions in the women's latrine.

Like Tanforan our living quarters had no partitions, no furniture, and no running water in the rooms, only a pot-bellied stove. One naked light bulb served an entire family. We slept on army cots covered with a few blankets, which proved to be completely inadequate during the harsh winters. Dust constantly streamed in from open cracks in the walls.

Whether we ate, argued, cried, laughed, or defecated, we did it in the company of others. There was no privacy whatsoever. It was especially trying for large families. Married couples often had to share one room, along with their parents and children. In order to create some sense of privacy, people scrounged around for scraps of lumber that the carpenters might have left in haste. Some internees cleverly fashioned food crates and boxes into partitions. Most people often resorted to simply hanging sheets or blankets to use as room dividers.

I understood then, as clearly as I do now, that the government meant for our surroundings to humiliate and degrade us.

Realizing our confinement at Topaz was going to be longer than at Tanforan, I knew I had to get a job to keep my sanity. A friend from my old hometown and a block manager, Kazuto Masuda, needed an assistant. Since Kazuto and I got along well, I accepted the position.[18]

As an assistant block manager I often attended meetings when Kazuto could not. With a wife and a couple of children, there were times when he needed extra money to help his family, so he'd volunteer to help local farmers harvest their crops.[19]

Block managers' meetings provided a forum where we'd air our grievances and try to improve the standard of living in camp. At these meetings I presented my particular block problems. I think in Topaz, at least, were it not for the block managers, conditions in our camp wouldn't have improved. Block managers were responsible for ensuring that people were as comfortable as possible. The people in my block understood and empathized with what we could and couldn't do because, as internees, we were all in the same situation. James Hirano was in charge of the block managers' headquarters. He effectively articulated our problems and concerns to the camp administrators, all of whom were Caucasian.

Internees ran day-to-day operations, such as working in the mess hall or the hospital.[20] Our wages averaged nineteen dollars a month for professionals, sixteen dollars a month for everyone else.[21] We worked more than forty hours a week, including Saturdays. Even the Japanese Americans doctors, who often performed major surgery and worked wonders with limited supplies and equipment, only earned nineteen dollars a month. Medicines and doctors always seemed to be in short supply.

Many of our most basic needs weren't met. We endured extreme temperatures — from ten to twenty degrees below zero in the brutal winter, to over one hundred degrees in the summer — without sufficient protection or relief. The frequent dust storms brought out asthma reactions in many internees. There was no escaping a dust storm. This same dust turned into sticky, miserable mud during the winter and rainy seasons. Given the dramatic shifts in temperature, we needed more essentials, like coal for our pot-bellied stoves during the winter. I remember one particular cold spell when I was assigned to distribute coal equally to everyone in my block. I stood for hours with shovel in hand as people brought their coal buckets to be filled. I had seventy-two compartments to tend to.

My mother's rheumatism improved slightly during the summers because of the warm desert climate. She was confined to the indoors during most of the winter, though, unable to walk very well in the cold and snow. In her usual fashion, she didn't complain.

The nutritional needs of the internees especially concerned us. Children, for example, didn't get adequate amounts of milk and fruits. Acquiring better meats became a priority for us, since we were only able to get liver, gizzard, tongue, tripe, brain, and chitterlings. It cost the government thirty-one to forty-five cents per meal to feed each person in camp.[22]

In Topaz, the block managers and assistant block managers helped plant vegetables to supplement the meals. One day I traveled with the other managers to an area just outside of our camp. We went there under guard in an Army truck. We spent a whole day — eight hours — doing back-breaking work under the hot sun. We hoed the ground and planted cabbage and other vegetables. It was torture. My face was beet red by the time we finished. All I wanted was to jump into a cool shower as soon as we got back to the camp; the long lines, however, made that wish impossible.

Improvements came slowly in the camps. As better qualities of meats arrived, we suspected that some administrative personnel engaged in black marketing, which further reduced our supply. We repeatedly complained to the project director about the situation, and eventually changes were made. The camp director was quite compassionate and did address many of our problems.

In time, some of the Caucasian personnel who got to know us came to trust us and empathized with our predicament. I got to know a few of them. Roscoe Bell became the assistant director of the camp and grew close to a number of Japanese Americans. His secretary was my future sister-in-law, Yo Kitashima. Mr. Bell liked Yo so much that he and his wife Gladys attended her wedding, which was held in the camp. I also remember Eleanor Gerard Sekerak, a camp teacher, and her husband Emil. The Sekeraks were warm and friendly people who befriended many of the internees. You would sometimes find Emil outside playing baseball with the internees. These individuals knew what we were up against and tried to make our lives a little easier. [23]

Our generation, the Nisei, came of age in the camps. We assumed more of a leadership role because most of the Issei were already well into their sixties. In that regard, the camps threw family life into upheaval. It was both easy and sad to see how family ties were strained or broken. Kids often ate at the mess halls with their friends rather than with their siblings or parents; that would've been unheard of in the outside community. Parents seemed powerless to assert authority when they themselves lacked control over their lives. Family life wasn't the same.

One of the necessary evils of camp life that I had a hard time getting used to were the long lines for everything. Waiting became second nature for us. We lined up to eat, to bathe, even to get our paychecks. The line for the canteen was especially long because goods were limited. I knew many women whose husbands stood in line to buy sanitary napkins for them so they'd have a double supply. Since there was only one bathtub for our whole block, there was usually a line for that. Because of the change in our diet, coupled with the stress of camp life, many people had diarrhea. It was terrible to have to wait in line with an upset stomach, but that was the way it was. We lined up for everything because there was never enough of anything. It took some time before I adjusted to this way of life. And before my life took on any sense of "normalcy," I found myself deeply frustrated. I held out hope that we would be released and allowed to go home in time for Christmas, my favorite time of the year. The year was 1943. It was purely wishful thinking on my part.

World War II raged on. The Allies won decisive victories in 1942–43. Japan suffered defeats at Midway and Guadalcanal; the Italians and Germans experienced defeats in North Africa. Mussolini's regime fell in mid-1943.

The ensuing months crept by. Many internees found diversions to pass time and maintain sanity. We watched old movies brought into Topaz and screened in the barracks; some people took up arts and crafts; younger internees played softball and other sports.

I would often go and watch my brothers and Tom Kitashima, a young man from my hometown, play softball in the evenings. My social life was rather limited, but I accepted it. I helped out in our camp's Buddhist Sunday School and felt good about that. On Sundays I would take some of the young children from my block to church. We had both Buddhist and

Christian services, as well as bilingual services. Both the English and Japanese language services usually attracted standing room-only audiences. It seemed we were all in search of spiritual guidance and comfort.

With thousands of people confined to a relatively small area, hidden talents quickly emerged. We had wonderful artists in Topaz, as well as people who simply had a knack for handicrafts. The results were mind-boggling. People created incredible objects from sagebrush roots, discarded orange and food crates, automobile springs, onion sacks, and shells. For example, it took one internee two years to make a fruit bowl that was ten inches in diameter and crafted out of sagebrush root. Using nothing more than a broken rice bowl as a tool, this man tediously carved the root. Some internees made beautiful dressers and furniture for their living quarters. Many creative and resourceful people among us made functional items out of throwaway materials.

I dabbled in some handicrafts, such as making leather key chains and small accessories. My girlfriends and I briefly took up knitting, a popular pastime in our camp. A number of us also made pieces of jewelry from shells we unearthed around the camp.

My brother Hiss put his talents to use, too. He was a skilled hair cutter and often went around Topaz cutting his friends' hair. Hiss had cut my hair when I was in grammar school. He outdid himself, though, when he built a beautiful *obutsudan* (Buddhist altar) out of orange crates he found around camp. Using empty fruit cans, he lined the inside of the *obutsudan*, giving it a sparkle of gold. He hand carved a lotus flower into the wood for a finishing touch. Out of kindness, my mother gave the *obutsudan* to a neighbor friend who didn't have one. To this day, I often wonder what happened to the altar. It was a work of art and a labor of love.

Despite these diversions, life in Topaz was not carefree and easy. People died in the camps, many from natural causes and some by suicide. A few were even killed at the hands of others.

On April 11, 1943, a fatal shooting occurred in Topaz. James Wakasa, a sixty-three-year-old bachelor, was killed by a camp guard. Shot in the chest, he died instantly. Rumors surfaced that Mr. Wakasa was shot simply because he had wandered too close to the perimeter fence.[24] Controversy and outrage erupted over the shooting. No one witnessed the shooting so several different accounts unfolded. The Army claimed Mr. Wakasa tried to escape, even though he died well inside the fenced area. Some internees believed he had tried to retrieve a dog that had gotten loose under the barbed wire fence. Another rumor circulated that he had merely been picking wildflowers near the fence and that when the guard ordered him to "Halt," he did not. According to those who knew him, Mr. Wakasa couldn't hear very well.

After the shooting, the commissary workers in our camp protested by striking for two days. Work stoppages occurred throughout the camp. The MPs arrived in armed jeeps as a show of force. The soldier responsible for the shooting supposedly went on trial but was found not guilty of any crime. He was transferred to another camp.

Because of the shooting, we became even more fearful of trigger-happy guards. We believed the rumors that most of the guards were soldiers recently released from the Army and purposely assigned to the various internment camps.[25]

I eventually gave up my assistant block manager's job to become the secretary to James Hirano, the head of the block managers. I took minutes at the block managers' meetings and then sent them on to the project director. I later accepted a job as the secretary to Claude Pratt, the head of community services. I enjoyed the work very much.

On a couple of occasions, I left Topaz as a seasonal laborer with several of my girlfriends, some of whom were from my block, some from my hometown. Utah farmers needed the labor, and it was a way for us to earn extra money. My friends generally enjoyed these leaves, but I didn't.

There was one instance when we helped pick cherries for a local grower. We were near the Salt Lake area in Ogden and in smaller neighboring towns. I remember we left Topaz in the midst of a hot summer. Picking cherries was tough work. Each of us had to haul a big ladder. There were other non-Japanese workers among us, and we learned that we were being paid less than them. That made us angry.

Soon after we began picking I felt feverish and noticed angry red welts sprouting on my limbs. Although I didn't know it right then, I was having a bad allergic reaction to ragweed, which grows wild in Utah. Unfortunately, there was no vehicle immediately available to take me back to the workers' camp. While I waited, someone suggested I lie down on the grass to make me feel better. It turned out the grass was also ragweed. By the time I got back to the workers' camp, my entire body was covered with huge welts.

It was around the Fourth of July. I recall that because we couldn't find a doctor anywhere. My friends tried to help out and applied calamine lotion all over my body. As night fell and the hours passed, I became increasingly uncomfortable and couldn't sleep a wink. The lotion was actually making me feel worse. I decided I had to take a shower and wash it off. There was a packing shed near our bunks where the male workers had erected a makeshift shower that we all used. I slipped out of the bunkhouse and headed to the shed. To my disappointment the water was stone cold. The soap wouldn't lather, and my efforts to rid myself of the lotion were to no avail. I was completely and utterly miserable. As soon as I was able to see a doctor, he immediately ordered me back to Topaz. That put an end to that leave.

The only other seasonal leave I volunteered for was to process and sort peas at a nearby food plant. I had to stand at a conveyor belt and sort out the good peas from the bad ones. We had to work quickly. Many of us — myself included — became ill, similar to a motion sickness, from staring at the fast-moving belt and the peas. That made me zero for two in the seasonal leave department.

A variety of outside businesses needed extra labor. Some internees helped pluck turkeys on turkey farms. A local alfalfa and hay grower who needed extra laborers hired my friend Tom Kitashima to cook meals for the work crew. Luckily for him, a number of the workers were his friends, and they ate whatever he cooked for them without complaining. The crew was often allowed to venture into town, so Tom enjoyed his leave.

In general many of us felt restless in camp and needed a change of pace, even if for a brief period. Some internees thrived on the outside and left Topaz indefinitely to move to the East Coast.[26] Several of my friends moved back east to attend beauty schools and ended up putting down roots there. I was a failure as far as going out to work. In Utah there were too few jobs and opportunities for women, and I wasn't adventurous enough to trek east to start a new life.

As the government became more lax about seasonal and temporary leaves, camp administrators allowed internees to shop in the nearby town of Delta. It was a tiny town, about a block long and with some fifteen hundred people. We went there under guard and in an Army vehicle. Every block in Topaz appointed a representative for the trip to be responsible for shopping for the entire block. My sister Lillian and I volunteered once to do this. We canvassed our block, taking orders for items people wanted. The list was endless: threads or buttons of a specific color, aspirin, candy, even meats. We thought it would be fun traveling into town, but I didn't volunteer to do it ever again.

It wasn't a leisurely trip at all. With so many people wanting specific and special items, we didn't want to disappoint anyone in our block. We had no time to ourselves, and felt overwhelmed trying to find all the things people requested. The stores in Delta — mainly bargain basement places — simply piled their goods high atop tables with no rhyme or reason to them. I had dreamed of going into a drugstore and drinking a milkshake, but there wasn't any time to do even that. We were completely worn out by the end of the trip.

On our way to Delta a funny incident occurred. We were riding along in an Army truck driven by an MP who had a list of everyone who was supposed to be in the truck. Along the way he came to a complete stop and decided to take roll call. He went down the list one by one, calling out our names and waiting for our replies. At the end of the list was the description, "one Caucasian," obviously referring to the MP himself. He called out, "Mr. Caucasian?" When no one answered, he got angry and demanded, "There's a Caucasian on this list. Where's Mr. Caucasian?" He asked this again and refused to move the truck until he got an answer. I guess he figured it out, because he finally started up the truck and continued on to Delta. All of us sitting behind him got a real bang out of that. The joke among us was that the MPs weren't very intelligent, and he certainly proved that. Wearing broad smiles, we all had a good laugh afterwards.

Immediately after the bombing of Pearl Harbor in 1941, all Japanese American men of draft age and those already serving in the military were reclassified as 4-C, or enemy aliens. Those in the military were summarily discharged, while those wanting to volunteer were denied entry. As the war in the Pacific escalated, however, the War Department reversed its policy and reinstated selective service for Japanese Americans beginning in January 1943.

A month later, all internees over the age of seventeen, both male and female, were asked to complete an ambiguous questionnaire entitled "Application for Leave Clearance." Every internee had to answer two crucial questions as ultimate proof of their allegiance.

Question #27: Are you willing to serve in the armed forces of the United States on combat duty, wherever ordered?

Question #28: Will you swear unqualified allegiance to the United States and faithfully defend the United States from any and all attack by foreign or domestic forces, and forswear any form of allegiance or obedience to the Japanese emperor or to any other foreign government, power, or organization?

Some internees considered the questionnaire a monumental insult, as though loyalty was something that could be quantified. The two questions generated great debate. Question #27 asked whether Japanese Americans were willing to fight for the United States, the very country that denied them their basic Constitutional rights and imprisoned them without due process guaranteed under the Bill of Rights. Question #28 was particularly problematic for the Issei; since the United States did not allow them to become naturalized American citizens, how could they swear their unqualified allegiance? The question drew outrage from Japanese Americans since many had never had an allegiance to any country other than America.

The "loyalty questionnaire," as it came to be known, which sought to weed out the "disloyal" among us, proved to be a divisive exercise. It generated enormous controversy and conflict within families and between individuals. Some parents had sons already serving in the military and so the questionnaire only created further uneasiness. It even split families apart.[27]

Those individuals who answered "No-No" to both questions #27 and #28 were segregated from the rest and sent to a maximum security camp called Tule Lake, near the Oregon border in Northern California. The military, rather than the WRA, ran Tule Lake, and so the atmosphere was much more prison-like than the other camps.

Understandably, there were those who answered in the negative even though they were loyal to, and loved, the United States. These individuals said they would not serve their country unless the government restored their Constitutional rights. People around camp argued that it was completely outrageous for Japanese aliens, like my parents, to register "unqualified allegiance" to America, a country which had legally barred them from becoming citizens. Forswearing any allegiance to Japan would essentially leave the Issei a people without a country.

My brothers were extremely upset that they, like other Japanese American men of draft age, had automatically been reclassified with "4-C" status after the Japanese bombed Pearl Harbor. My mother voiced concerns about what would happen to our family if my brothers were drafted and then killed in battle. Many parents worried that the military would consider their sons expendable because of their ethnicity and therefore would place them in "suicide squads." With such an uncertain future before them, and after a great deal of soul-searching, my three brothers decided to answer "No-No." They were sent to Tule Lake. My mother, my sister Nobuko, and her husband, also responded with "No-No" and joined them. Over one thousand people in our camp answered as they did.[28] Like my brothers, Tom [Kitashima] was also frustrated and angry about the questionnaire. He initially intended to answer "No-No," but people in his block talked him out of doing that.

Women had to sign a statement whether they would voluntarily serve with the WAACs (Women's Auxiliary Army Corps) or the Army Nurse Corps. I answered "Yes-Yes" to the questions.

Lillian and her husband, who was too old to serve in the armed forces, and their daughter Connie, remained in Topaz. I stayed behind with them. My mother didn't force me to go with the rest of the family to Tule Lake. I think she took comfort in knowing that Lillian and I would remain together.

We corresponded with my mother and siblings after that, but Lillian and I worried a great deal about them. No one knew the fate of people being sent to Tule Lake. As difficult as it was for me to be separated from the rest of my family, that was the choice I had made.

Japanese Americans Serve with Distinction in World War II [29]

Over thirty-three thousand Japanese Americans served in the U.S. armed forces in World War II. Initially disallowed from enlisting or remaining in military service, an all-Japanese American battalion—the 100th Infantry Battalion—was formed in Hawai`i in May 1942. They were later joined by their mainland counterparts, Japanese Americans who volunteered from the detention camps to serve in the segregated 442nd Regimental Combat Team. Together, the 100th Battalion and 442nd RCT became the most decorated unit in U.S. military history for its size and length of service.

One particular battle of note was the 442nd RCT's rescue of the Texan "Lost Battalion" (First Battalion, 141st Regiment, 36th Division), who were surrounded by enemy fire in France's Vosges Mountains. The 442nd ultimately prevailed after a week of intense fighting, but at great sacrifice: In saving two hundred and eleven men of the "Lost Battalion," they suffered over eight hundred casualties, including one hundred and eighty four dead.

Ironically, it was a Japanese American unit, the 522nd Field Artillery Battalion of the 442nd, that was among the first American troops to liberate the Dachau concentration camps in Germany in April 1945.

Thousands of Japanese American soldiers also played a decisive and critically important role in the U.S. Army's Military Intelligence Service, serving as interpreters, interrogators, and translators, and providing key intelligence support to every major theater of the war, particularly in the Pacific. Major General Charles Willoughby, General Douglas MacArthur's chief of intelligence G-2, credited the MIS for having "saved countless lives and shortened the war by two years."

By war's end, the 100th Battalion and 442nd RCT had participated in eight major campaigns in Europe, earning, among other distinctions, over eighteen thousand individual decorations for bravery and more than nine thousand Purple Hearts.

The 100/442nd RCT was welcomed home in 1946 by President Harry Truman, who presented them with their eighth Presidential Distinguished Unit Citation and said, "You fought for the free nations of the world — you fought not only the enemy, you fought prejudice — and you won."

V

STARTING OVER

With President Roosevelt's reelection safely in hand, and a decision rendered by the United States Supreme Court that there was no legal basis for continuing to detain citizens against their will, Japanese Americans were allowed to re-enter the West Coast beginning in January 1945. America's concentration camps began closing that same year. The Topaz camp officially closed on October 31, 1945; Tule Lake closed in March 1946, the last of the ten camps to do so.

My experiences as an assistant block manager taught me about people and dealing with difficult situations. I think my sense of activism started back then. When the government began closing the camps, several people in my block expressed concern and anxiety.

A woman with two young children and a husband serving in the military sought my help. She wanted her husband discharged, so that he could help her and the children resettle. An elderly couple in my block had a son serving in the military. They need-ed his help in the resettlement because the father was a stroke victim and the mother was in poor health. Their only other child, a daughter, spoke no English. They worried that upon their release from the camps their daughter would be unable to find work and help care for them. They were genuinely con-cerned about their survival and refused to leave Topaz, declaring they would remain out of protest. "You put us in here and left us with nothing to go back to," they told the camp administrators. Social workers pleaded with this couple to reconsider.

I finally decided to intervene and write on behalf of these two families to the respective commanding officers for the husband's and son's release from the Army. I don't know whether my letters had any impact, but to our amazement, the two men were released and reunited with their families.

On August 11, 1945, I married Tom Kitashima in Salt Lake City. Tom came from my hometown of Centerville and had worked for a potato farmer there. Our two families were close. He and I had been seeing each other for about nine years.

We shared a love of sports and community activities. He was a left-handed pitcher for the Washington Union High School baseball team, our alma mater. We had been members of the Washington township JACL and participated in many of its events together. Tom was an amiable and likable person. At some of our community get togethers, he would sing "Red Sails in the Sunset," one of his favorite songs. He had a really nice singing voice.

While in Topaz, Tom worked as a stock clerk in the mess hall. By the time we got married in August, the government was more lenient about letting internees travel, and so we left Topaz temporarily for Salt Lake City. It was rather frightening to be there at that time, however, because Japan's surrender was imminent. Businesses in the city began closing in anticipation of the celebration, and people were out in force decorating the streets. We didn't feel comfortable and were worried about finding a place to stay. Fortunately, we looked up a local friend whose family had lived in Tom's block. They ran a restaurant, so we ate all of our meals with them. Ours was a short honeymoon. We stayed just one night in Salt Lake City before returning to camp. People in our blocks were very surprised to see us back so soon. They figured we'd take advantage of the leave and stay for a week, but we were too afraid.

As Topaz neared closure, my supervisor Claude Pratt asked me to remain behind to help type up reports. The Pratts had been awfully nice to me and had helped make my confinement bearable. Mr. Pratt truly had compassion for Japanese Americans. He had even once requested, and received, permission from camp administrators to take Tom and me out to dinner and a cowboy movie in Delta with his wife and son. It was a rare treat. He had accepted full responsibility for doing this. We had received our share of stares from the townspeople, and I felt very self conscious about it. Thankfully we hadn't encountered any problems. I felt I owed him my help, plus I could gain civil service status from the job.

If I accepted the offer, though, Tom couldn't stay on at Topaz unless he also had a job. Unfortunately, there were no jobs for him. I mulled it over and finally decided to turn down Mr. Pratt's offer so that Tom and I could resettle together. Mr. Pratt completely understood my decision.

I experienced mixed emotions about leaving Topaz, because I had developed a bond with the people in my block. Not a one had been unkind to me. I'm sure many other internees also had conflicting feelings about leaving. It meant having to start over with nothing. If each of us knew exactly where we were headed and what we were going to do after we left Topaz, maybe leaving would've made everyone ecstatic. Instead, we were filled with uncertainty. After having been denied our liberty and freedom for such a long time, most of us weren't sure how to pick up the pieces of our lives again. Tom and I had no place of our own to return to, and we were concerned about where and how we would live. All we had was a sense of hope.

Fortunately for us, Lillian and her family had left Topaz before us. They had headed back to Northern California — San Francisco, to be exact — and were going to try and find us a place to stay upon our return. With the thought of being reunited with our families, Tom and I left Topaz, Utah, on September 20,

1945. We each received twenty-five dollars to begin our lives anew.[30] Mr. Pratt sent us off with blankets to keep us warm on our train ride. We headed home.

Several of our hometown friends relocated to Chicago and other places in the Midwest, where many still reside today. We were anxious about whether Californians would welcome us back, yet we never considered living outside of California. Tom didn't want to go to the Midwest; we had no roots anywhere else. California was our home. When we finally arrived back in Northern California, Tom and I didn't settle in Centerville. The home that my father had built on leased land had since been torn down. Nothing remained there for us. Some of our friends had resettled in parts of the East Bay, such as Richmond, where wartime housing was available to returning Japanese Americans. We opted instead to move to San Francisco. I had never lived in the city before.

The transition was rough. Lillian did her best to help us, but housing was very scarce in the city. The best she could find for her own family had been a storefront owned by a Japanese fellow on Buchanan Street. Her family and a couple of other families moved in there. Camp administrators had told us that housing would be plentiful, and that churches and other organizations would offer us shelter. That wasn't true. The only place available to Japanese Americans was in the Hunter's Point area, a ship-building area and former Army facility located far south of downtown. Housing once used by ship workers stood vacant, so Japanese Americans were allowed to stay there. Without a car, however, it was too far to live, especially if we wanted to find work downtown.

On our first night of freedom, Tom and I slept at the Japanese Buddhist Temple in San Francisco. The temple had been converted into a makeshift hostel for Japanese Americans, especially single men. There were few alternatives, other than living in storefronts or sharing boarding rooms with strangers.

Tom and I initially slept in the temple's movie projection room. The health department, though, soon ordered us out because the room, which had no windows, violated health regulations. We then moved to the balcony section of the temple, where we were crammed together with other married couples. We slept on army cots and hung blankets for partitions. Sleeping there, however, became dangerous after someone threw a rock through a nearby window, shattering glass everywhere. The only place left to move was downstairs.

I ended up sharing a small Sunday School classroom with a couple of other families and their children. Whenever I'd come in late at night I had to creep around so as not to awaken the children. It was an awkward arrangement, so Tom opted to sleep on a cot on the floor of the nearby gymnasium with about thirty other men. Some of them were also separated from their families, while others were bachelors. The gymnasium was icy cold and very noisy because every sound was amplified. I don't know how Tom could sleep. When we were in the projection room, which was located in the gymnasium, you could hear people talking, coughing, snoring, or getting up to use the bathroom. On top of that, the clogs that people had worn in camp made a distinct clomping sound across the hard floor. Sleep was hard to come by. To this day I can still hear the collective snoring of the men on that gymnasium floor, sounding very much like an orchestra tuning up.

It wasn't an ideal situation, but the temple gave us a roof over our heads for which we were enormously grateful. We lived off of government-issued food rations and pooled together our ration stamps with those of my sister's family and a couple of other families. We ate our meals with them rather than at the temple. In many ways, Tom and I had it easier than others because it was just the two of us. I felt sorry for families, especially those with small children or elderly parents, having to live like this after enduring the camps.

We eventually found a place of our own. A friend of ours and a former San Franciscan, Shizu Takahashi, knew people in the area and called them on our behalf. Some of her friends had homes with basements and rooms converted into makeshift apartments. We rented a unit on Bush Street, with its tiny kitchen and living room, and a good-sized bedroom. It felt like a palace.

Tom and I both found work in San Francisco. At first Tom had a difficult time, because he had no work experience other than farming. He finally landed a job with the WRA warehouse, where he handled the stored property of former internees. The WRA was the agency responsible for the administration and closing of the camps. Following the closure of the warehouse, Tom began his lifetime employment with a plastic bottling company in San Francisco.

With a letter of recommendation in hand from Mr. Pratt, I quickly landed a job at the regional office of the WRA, which was located downtown at First and Market Streets. I'm thankful that I didn't have to pound the pavement like many returning Japanese Americans were forced to do. I was given a head start.

In my work at the WRA, I learned firsthand that most of the items that Japanese Americans had entrusted to the government for storage prior to the evacuation had been either vandalized or stolen.[31] Government officials claimed that nothing could be done, which only made matters worse. Yet again, justice wasn't on our side.

Some communities didn't welcome, or want, us back. Violence and harassment were commonplace. A friend of mine owned a barn that was deliberately torched. The police apprehended two men who admitted responsibility for the crime, but the judge deemed them innocent. We heard of families who had stored personal belongings and expensive appliances, like refrigerators and stoves, in places like schoolhouses, only to return home and find these buildings destroyed. Their lifetime possessions were gone.

When our family contacted the police in our hometown to reclaim the cameras and radios we had been ordered to turn in, the police informed us that they had no records of these items. We couldn't prove they even existed. One of my sisters was furious and blurted out to the officers, "If we can't trust you, who can we trust?"

In addition to the WRA, I worked for a number of other agencies, such as the Sugar Rationing Board. These temporary jobs lasted about four or five months until ultimately all of the wartime agencies closed. After that, I took the civil service exam and landed a secretarial job with the Veteran's Administration (VA) in downtown San Francisco. Not too long afterwards, I became pregnant and decided to quit work in order to take care of our baby.

Our only child Alan was born on September 16, 1949. We were overjoyed with his birth; our families were equally ecstatic. I didn't go back to full-time work until Alan entered junior high school. Tom and I somehow made do on one salary and, in retrospect, I'm glad for the time I spent with Alan during those early years.

While he was just a youngster, I realized that World War II had an impact on his generation even though we didn't really talk about the war and our own experiences. I remember an occasion when Alan was playing with some of his friends. They wanted to play a game of war but couldn't get it started because no one wanted to be the Japanese, identified as the "bad guys." It was both funny and sad.

As Alan grew older, Tom and I became active in the local Boy Scouts of America. I served as a den mother for a few years. We tried to support Alan in all that he did. Like his dad, he loved baseball and went on to do quite well as a pitcher for Galileo High School. He continued playing baseball in the local Optimist League and in the Nikkei (Japanese American) Softball League.

The three of us did everything together. We particularly enjoyed going to football games. Tom was a diehard fan of the

San Francisco '49ers, and we watched them play at Kezar Stadium, their old home field. Come rain or shine, we went to every single game for four years straight. We really loved the team.

When I decided to return to work, I went back to the VA, where I staffed the reception desk at an outpatient clinic. The clinic and the downtown VA office eventually merged with the Ft. Miley Veteran's Administration Medical Center. I subsequently worked for the hospital's outpatient clinic for many years and later moved to a job in the eligibility section.

Members of both Tom and my families initially went their separate ways after the camps closed. Tom's mother, a widow who never remarried, moved back to the East Bay. His only brother Roy and his wife Yo, who were married in camp, initially resettled in Cleveland, Ohio. They later made their way back to Northern California. Tom had a couple of sisters as well. One, Margaret Ouye, resides in Northern California.

Since Tule Lake was the last camp to close, my family's return to freedom was delayed. During the time that we were separated as a family, I kept in touch through Hiss. He'd write and tell me what was happening with everyone. I learned that my brothers still kept up with their music playing and baseball.

Many of the Tule Lake internees who moved back to the Bay Area relocated to a housing area in Richmond, located across the bay and northward from San Francisco. My older brother Masao and younger brother James lived with my mother in Richmond. Hiss, though, left from Tule Lake and headed straight for New York, where he found work as a dental technician. We stayed in close touch. Unfortunately, because Tom and I didn't own a car and couldn't afford to buy one, we didn't get to see my mother and brothers very often. Occasionally, though, we'd take the bus to visit them. It wasn't an easy trip to make; we had to walk a long way from the bus stop to the housing area.

Nobuko and her husband Tom also moved back to the Bay Area, where she found domestic work in Alameda. Her husband had lived in Alameda for many years prior to the war and wanted to return there. He worked as a baker for the Southern Pacific railroad. It was Nobuko who scrimped and saved the money she made and eventually bought a home for them there. Lillian and her family settled in San Francisco, where she found employment with a jeweler.

When Hiss wrote to tell me he was returning to Northern California, he asked if I would help him find a place to live. That wasn't easy given the housing shortage, but luck was with us and I found him a place in Oakland. A Japanese family had agreed to let my brother stay with them for awhile. Hiss returned and eventually found work at a plastics company that produced neon signs for numerous Nevada casinos.

Thinking back on those years, Tom and I and both of our families tried as best we could to get on with our lives. In many ways it was a miracle that we survived through it all. We didn't have anything except for the twenty-five dollars each of us received to start over again. Starting over proved difficult. Our communities had to be rebuilt and Japanese American organizations reborn.

In the post-camp and resettlement years, my siblings and I, like any other family, experienced our share of hardships and sadness.

On April 16, 1968, my mother died of natural causes at the age of eighty-nine. She never talked much about the camps after we resettled in Northern California. I never heard her express any bitterness about those years, but then again she hardly complained, period. And, too, there wasn't really a time when we got together and talked about the camps and our feelings. Maybe that was more the norm than the exception. Many Issei never talk about that period of their lives. My mother was one of them. She dealt with pain with silence. At the time of her death she was not a naturalized U.S. citizen.[32]

Although all of us loved our mother, it was really Nobuko who had taken care of her. Nobuko didn't drive, so she would ride the bus from her home in Alameda to visit our mother in Richmond, a distance of nearly twenty miles. When our mother's arthritis became quite severe, she relented and agreed to go and live with Nobuko and her family.

Nobuko also looked out for each of her siblings. She was not only a devoted daughter but a loving sister as well. She never attended high school. Instead she went to work at a young age to help out the family. She worked hard, saved as much money as she could, and managed to buy a house prior to the evacuation, which she was forced to sell after the war broke out. After the camps, she continued to work and save and was able to buy another house, paying cash for it. She always offered to help me and my brothers and sister. She once tried to give Tom and me money to buy a house, but we refused it because we wanted to do it on our own. That was Nobuko. She passed away in 1992, ironically on April 16, the same date my mother died. I felt as though I had lost a mother all over again.

Cancer claimed my sister-in-law, James's wife, at a young age. She was carrying one of their children, a son, at the time of her death, but miraculously the baby was born healthy. James was left to raise their four children alone and did a remarkable job.

After the war, James worked for Simmons Mattress, where he was responsible for testing electric beds for use in hospitals. The job required a lot of out-of-state travel. It was trying for him, especially with a newborn, but he was determined to keep the family together, rejecting the suggestions of a few well-meaning friends that he place some of the children in foster homes. My mother, siblings and I pitched in to help whenever we could. I remember the long list of "reminders" that James had posted on the inside of their front door. There were instructions for the children. Each item was numbered: One. Be sure the stove is turned off. Two. Turn off the water. Three. Don't forget to take your lunch. It was as though my brother was there to send them off each day, even when he couldn't be. Seeing the list always brought tears to my eyes.

Masao never married. He had taken a liking to a girl from our hometown but nothing ever materialized. After that I think he simply lost interest in finding a wife. He had a steady job doing cabinetry work and saved a fair amount of money. He lived with my mother in Richmond and spent most of his life with her. Masao died on August 3, 1984.

Hiss married, had a son, and continued working at the plastics company until his retirement. He then worked part-time for Adachi Nursery in El Cerrito. He enjoyed that job immensely because of his fondness for gardening. He loved working with his hands and creating elaborate things, like detailed, inch-high *kokeshi* (wooden dolls). Hiss spent a good portion of his free time building a beautiful and natural Japanese garden in his yard. It had a *koi* (carp) pond and a handmade bridge. When a heart attack claimed Hiss's life on September 12, 1988, it was a shock and a tremendous loss for us all. I'll always remember him as a happy person who could make people laugh. His death was a blow to me because of our closeness. There were countless times when I called him just to talk. I miss him terribly even now.

Alan's and my life changed dramatically in 1975. By then, Alan, who was twenty-six, had moved out of our house and in with two of his buddies. Since most of his friends were already living apart from their families, we had given him our blessing. Tom became seriously ill that year. He was rushed to a hospital emergency room. The doctors decided to keep him there overnight to run some tests. The following day passed slowly. I remember it well.

Alan suspected something was terribly wrong and called me at work that day. "What's wrong with dad?" he asked. I had no answer for him since I myself didn't know.

After I got home from work that afternoon, the phone rang. It was Tom's doctor. He gently explained to me that Tom had liver cancer and that it was only a matter of time. I was completely devastated. "How could this be?" I screamed over the phone. There had been no warning, no evidence that something was gravely wrong. But the doctor was certain. The most difficult thing for me was telling Alan. When I saw him that evening I told him as bravely as I could that his father was dying of cancer. We just held each other and cried.

Tom was so much like my mother because he could tolerate a lot of physical pain without showing it or complaining about it. I think that might've ultimately led to his condition. Even if he experienced severe pain, he wouldn't say anything. He was an otherwise healthy person despite having had two earlier operations for an ulcer. He must've been suffering for some time but hid it well from us.

The doctor quickly admitted Tom to the hospital. Alan moved back home. I spent everyday thereafter at the hospital with Tom. I tried to be useful by helping the nurses change his bedding and doing whatever I could to assist them. The nurses were wonderful, and their constant concern touched me. The same can be said for Tom's doctor. One day he pulled me aside and asked me what Tom's favorite wine was. He said he wanted to buy him a bottle for being such a wonderful patient. He told me it was an honor to be Tom's doctor because he had never had a patient who faced pain with such dignity. I thanked him for his kindness and felt fortunate we had such a dedicated and compassionate caregiver.

The cancer spread quickly to Tom's lungs and kidneys, and even though we knew there was no hope, his death hit us hard. He died on April 4, 1975. I'm relieved that he at least knew of Alan's graduation from San Francisco State University before he died. On his deathbed he called for Alan, saying he was sorry that he was going to die without leaving us anything. Alan comforted and reassured him, and said, "You gave us everything, dad. And don't worry about mom, I'll look after her."

Tom's mother, who lived across the bay in Berkeley, was grief-stricken. After his death, we talked nearly every night for hours, consoling one another. She talked about the trauma of losing a child and said it sometimes gave her comfort to talk to Tom aloud, as if he were still there. She had been as strong as an ox up until his death. Then her health began to slowly deteriorate and she passed away several years later in May, 1981.

Not long after Tom's death, a woman from a federal agency in Washington, D.C. contacted me. I can't recall her name but she explained that she worked on issues of aging and expressed an interest in interviewing Japanese American widows for a story she was writing.

I don't know how she got my telephone number, perhaps from one of the Japanese American organizations. Talking with this woman made me feel better. We spoke for nearly an hour. When she asked me how I was coping with Tom's death, I told her that the emptiness I felt was sometimes so overwhelming that I wanted to go to Ocean Beach when no one was around and scream and cry at the top of my lungs.

Fortunately I had a job to keep me busy. The hardest times came at night when I returned home to our six-room flat. It felt empty. Mealtimes were especially difficult; for a time, eating itself became mechanical. I found myself swallowing food down quickly, not even tasting it, or else I knew I wouldn't be able to eat at all. In the back of my mind, I knew I had to keep my strength up or risk becoming ill myself. A girlfriend of mine, who was also widowed, told me that she ate her meals standing over the kitchen sink, shoveling the food into her mouth and not knowing whether she would be able to keep it down. I could really relate to that.

My family and friends helped fill the void after Tom's death. My dear friends Masako Nishimura and Toshiko Hosoda provided great comfort during those lonely times. Harry and Lucy Konda would invite me over for dinner whenever I needed to talk to someone. Only a person who experiences this kind of loss can understand the deep loneliness that ensues. The wonderful support of friends like these continues even today.

The opportunities I soon had to volunteer in the community were like an elixir for me. Volunteering gave me a boost and kept me busy. I continued working at the VA hospital, telling my boss that I would die working and with my boots on. With the issuance of new regulations, however, I was forced to retire in 1981. It was then that I devoted myself full time to community volunteer work and to the redress and reparations campaign for Japanese Americans.

VI

QUEST FOR JUSTICE

In the 1970s third generation Japanese Americans — the Sansei — learning of the gross injustices their parents and grandparents endured, raised their voices to question and challenge the constitutionality of the U.S. government's actions during World War II. As more Americans learned about the wartime internment, calls to rectify this grievous wrong grew louder and stronger. What happened to Japanese Americans should never happen again to any group of people simply because of race or ancestry, they said. The campaign for redress and reparations had begun.

Garnering public support for the grassroots movement took years. Educating the Japanese American community itself was an important first step so that the community could be united in its quest for justice. Organizations such as the Japanese American Citizens League, the National Coalition for Redress and Reparations, and the National Council for Japanese American Redress ,[33] all played important roles in advancing the struggle for redress and reparations.

Broadcast and print media served to bring this issue before the nation's conscience. People of all races, religions, and ages who believed in justice joined in, proclaiming that this was a national and historical wrong that needed to be corrected. Constitutional and academic scholars echoed this, acknowledging that the internment was one of the worst violations of constitutional rights in our country's history for Japanese Americans had not only lost physical property and possessions, but also liberty and freedom, jobs, and economic and educational opportunities.

I wanted to be a part of the struggle for redress and reparations, to right this wrong, so I became involved with the National Coalition for Redress and Reparations in 1980, the year in which it was founded. I wanted most of all to educate the general public about the truth of what happened during the war, even though each time I spoke about my experience, it brought back dark memories.

National Coalition for Redress and Reparations (NCRR)

Community-minded Sansei in California organized the NCRR. It began as a pro-gressive coalition of the Committee for Redress, the Little Tokyo People's Rights Organization, which challenged the evictions caused by redevelopment of the Little Tokyo area of Los Angeles back in the 1970s, the Japanese Community Progressive Alliance, and the San Jose Nihonmachi Outreach Committee, a community based organization dedicated to public education about the internment. A grass-roots organization, NCRR's purpose is to uphold the constitutional, civil, and human rights of Japanese Americans, Asian/Pacific Islanders, and all Americans. NCRR supports those who have suffered, or still suffer, from injustice and racism, and con-tinues to work toward the social, cultural, and political empowerment of all com-munities. The membership of NCRR-San Francisco grew to about three hundred with chapters in Los Angeles and San Jose as well. In 2000, the Los Angeles Chapter of NCRR changed its name to Nikkei for Civil Rights and Redress and con-tinues its active participation in the civil rights arena.

Landmark Commission on Wartime Relocation and Internment of Civilians (CWRIC) Hearings

On July 31, 1980, President Jimmy Carter signed into law P.L. 96-317, which created the Commission on Wartime Relocation and Internment of Civilians (CWRIC). The nine-member Commission — with three members each appointed by the President, the House, and the Senate — was charged with reviewing the facts and circumstances surrounding Executive Order 9066 and the internment of Japanese Americans, and recommending appropriate remedies.

Beginning in July 1981, and over the next year and a half, the Commission held hearings in nine cities. Over seven hundred and fifty witnesses, the majority of whom were Japanese Americans, testified. [34]

Along with my good friend Lillian Kiyota, I attended NCRR's first meeting in 1980 in preparation for the CWRIC hearing in San Francisco. I had read about the meeting in the

Hokubei Mainichi, a Japanese American daily newspaper in San Francisco, and probably like countless others, I wondered how in the world this younger generation of Japanese Americans thought they could spur our government on to address a decades-old issue.

About seventy-five people attended this meeting. Sansei leaders — such as Marlene Tonai and Naomi Kubota — who took the initiative in trying to educate our community and raise interest in the Commission hearings, vigorously appealed to former internees to testify. The meeting started off slowly. Many of us Nisei weren't used to speaking in public at all, let alone about such personal feelings and experiences. I also think people were hesitant about saying anything negative about our government for fear of retribution.

The Sansei persisted, though. The hearings, they said, represented a unique opportunity to address a select group of people. It was an important and major stepping stone, one which Japanese Americans couldn't afford to ignore. I looked at these Sansei with amazement. They had nothing to gain by this, and yet they were so determined and committed. Lillian and I decided that as former internees we had a duty to testify. We both signed up. It would be my first opportunity to tell of my experiences after almost forty years.

The San Francisco hearings were held on August 11-13, 1981, at Golden Gate University. The moment I opened the door of the auditorium and saw the capacity crowd of over six hundred people, tears welled in my eyes and a huge lump formed in my throat. It was overwhelming to see such interest from people of all different ages and races, people who had come to listen to what we had to say. I was especially delighted to see young students with papers and pen in hand, busily taking notes of this historic occasion. Scores of people would learn first-hand about the trauma of the evacuation and internment, and about the emotional and psychological scars that remained.

The atmosphere in that auditorium resembled a premiere event. Cameras flashed nonstop throughout the hearing. Translators provided information for those who spoke Japanese. The room was also equipped with earphones for Issei who were hearing impaired. A slew of newspaper reporters as well as TV crews from both Japan and America attended. Media coverage of the hearings truly played a crucial and significant role in helping to educate the general public about the camps.

The members of the blue-ribbon Commission were all very distinguished people.[35] Judge Marutani presided over this hearing because the chair, Joan Bernstein, was absent.

Unfortunately, having public hearings also attracted bigots and racists. There are people who still cannot, or will not, differentiate between Japanese nationals and Japanese Americans. Lillian Baker, a vocal and active opponent of redress and reparations from Southern California, had tried her best to disrupt an earlier commission hearing. About a week before, she attended the hearing in Los Angeles and walked up to the table where a former internee was testifying. She grabbed the material from this person's hands and tore it up. We were on the alert for her to appear at this hearing; a security guard was posted at the door.

Indeed, Lillian Baker did appear. I was seated near the door when she entered. She tried to be clever: rather than head straight down the aisle, she walked along the perimeter of the auditorium along the last row of seats before working her way toward the table where people were about to testify. The security guard intercepted her before she got close enough and removed her from the premises. Despite this minor disruption, the hearings went smoothly and Baker did little to dampen the spirits of those willing to share their stories.

I attended all three hearing days. Listening to so many moving testimonies somehow made my own experiences seem less painful. A mother with two small children told of her terrifying experience in the aftermath of Pearl Harbor. Military police searched her home, making shambles of her family's possessions, knocking pictures off the walls, cutting up mattresses, smashing a Buddhist altar to pieces. Then they waited for her husband to return home only so they could take him away. Afterwards, her children were too traumatized to sleep alone.

With each passing day, the time allotted for individual testimony was shortened in order to accommodate all the people — over one hundred — who wanted to speak. People from as far away as Reno, Nevada, Sacramento and other parts of Northern California were eager to have their say. Our community viewed that as a great sign.

I testified on the last days of the hearings. By then, each speaker had four minutes. After the first two days of the hearings I went home and practiced my testimony over and over, timing myself to make sure I stayed within the time limit. I found it impossible to say everything I wanted, and agonized over how to collapse almost three-and-a-half years of my life into four short minutes.

I spoke about the humiliation of being fed discolored cold cuts, overcooked swiss chard and moldy bread. I told of my brother's losses as a farmer, the horror of being placed in a horse-stall with manure on the floor, hay-filled mattresses that served as our beds, the lack of privacy, the terrible sanitation, and the irony of holding memorial services for our Japanese American soldiers while behind barbed wire fences.

My only regret about the hearing is that Congressman Dan Lungren left early with very little participation on his part. He said he had other business to attend to. As a presidential appointee to the Commission, the hearing should've been his primary focus for those three days. He had a duty and an obligation to the President and the Commission. The fact that Mr. Lungren had been quite vocal about his feelings regarding reparations — he felt the government wouldn't support redress — didn't sit well with many of us. It seemed as though he didn't care to listen to what we had to say. What really upset me then was that no one on the Commission or in our community questioned his actions. I'm mad at myself as well. I didn't have the courage then, but if that happened today I would've said, "Now just a minute, Mr. Lungren..." It wasn't right.

With an overflow of people wanting to testify late in the hearings, there wasn't enough time to hear them all. One of the commission members, Dr. Arthur Flemming, however, was very sympathetic and gracious. He set aside an evening at a local church to listen to those who wanted to share their stories. During the official hearings he had remarked that learning about what happened to Japanese Americans during the war was one of the greatest history lessons he had ever learned.

Letter-Writing Campaign

The NCRR chapters (Los Angeles, San Francisco, San Jose) and their supporters vigorously embarked on letter-writing campaigns to educate the public and members of Congress about the internment.

I became thoroughly involved in this campaign, carrying pre-printed letters addressed to members of Congress and the President for people to sign. I carried these wherever I went, so that they became, along with my purse, a part of my everyday attire. Our local NCRR members tirelessly distributed and collected signed letters at community events, churches, street fairs, schools, and other places where Japanese Americans gathered, and then brought them to me for mailing. We enlisted the help of other friends and community people[36] who deserve considerable thanks for their tremendous efforts in collecting hundreds of letters to send to Congress. These special folks took letters to their friends, to churches, bowling alleys, even golf courses. They patiently explained the importance of these letters to anyone willing to listen.

Full of talented, hard-working people, the NCRR–San Francisco chapter was fortunate to have members[37] and friends willing to do grassroots work. John Ota, a Sansei and longtime community activist, did a wonderful job penning our letters and various articles. We did a lot of things with very little money. My apartment became NCRR's office and headquarters since we couldn't afford to rent office space.

In February 1983, the Commission issued Personal Justice Denied, its four hundred and sixty-seven page report to Congress. The Commission unanimously concluded that the exclusion, detention and internment of Japanese Americans were not a result of military necessity. Instead, they were a result of "race prejudice, war hysteria and a failure of political leadership." No Japanese or Japanese American in the United States was ever charged with, or found guilty of, sabotage or disloyalty during or after the war, thereby negating the justification of "military necessity." For the first time, an official government voice acknowledged the wrongfulness of the internment: it was neither justified nor necessary to evacuate and intern Japanese Americans during World War II.

Six months later, the Commission issued its recommendations and enumerated several remedies, including compensation in the amount of twenty thousand dollars to each eligible individual, an official government apology, and the establishment of an education fund. Representative Lungren was the lone member of the nine-member Commission who opposed individual monetary compensation.

In the early stages of the redress campaign, I used to type or handwrite the addresses on each and every envelope after collecting a stack of letters. Sometimes I would write the addresses straight up and down, or slanted to the left, or slanted to the right, trying to change the look of my handwriting. I know it was silly but I wanted each envelope to look personal and unique. We even used postage stamps with the word "LOVE" imprinted on them. We were willing to try anything and everything to touch members of Congress!

The floor of my apartment was usually blanketed with letters and envelopes as I folded, addressed, sealed, and stamped each one. Everyday I took letters to the Kimochi nutrition site, a senior lunch program where I volunteer, and distributed them to participants.

I often asked the other volunteers to assist in collecting letters. I once timed myself and was able to collect one hundred and ten signed letters in ten minutes!

All of us in the NCRR worked to convince members of Congress and the general public of the importance of rectifying this dark chapter in America's history. We had to make them realize that when the Constitutional rights of one group of people are violated, the rights of all Americans are jeopardized.

Introduction of the First Redress Bill: 1983

In order to fully implement the recommendations of the CWRIC, House Majority Leader Jim Wright introduced H.R. 4110 on October 6, 1983. In the Senate, Spark Matsunaga introduced S. 2116 on November 16, 1983. These bills sought to implement fully the Commission's recommendations. Given the conservative climate and opposition from key subcommittee and committee chairs in the ninety-eighth Congress, both bills failed to make it out of committee.

***Coram Nobis* Cases**

Attempts to address the injustices and wrongfulness of the internment also occurred in another venue: the courts. Three landmark cases, known as the coram nobis cases, had a major and positive impact on the redress effort. They proved no legal justification existed for the evacuation and internment.

In the 1940s, three Japanese Americans — Fred Korematsu, Minoru Yasui, and Gordon Hirabayashi — individually challenged the constitutionality of the wartime orders during World War II. They lost. The United States Supreme Court ultimately heard their cases and upheld their convictions and the constitutionality of the evacuation and internment.

In 1942, Min Yasui, a lawyer, Army officer and Japanese American community leader in Oregon, challenged the legality of the curfew and evacuation orders by deliberately violating curfew. He served nine months in prison. In Seattle, Gordon Hirabayashi, a Quaker, violated curfew and exclusion orders on moral grounds. He was arrested and convicted. In San Leandro, California, Fred Korematsu failed to report for evacuation. In love with a Caucasian woman, he avoided internment to be with her, even undergoing minor plastic surgery to alter his appearance. Following his arrest and conviction, Korematsu spent time in jail before being sent to Tanforan detention center.

In 1983, a legal team comprised of Sansei attorneys and Professor Peter Irons of the University of California, San Diego, filed a petition for <u>writ of error coram nobis</u> to have all three cases reopened. This rarely—invoked legal procedure address-es cases of fundamental error or manifest injustice, such as when those convicted have already served time. Irons and Ms. Aiko Herzig-Yoshinaga, a researcher and former internee, had discovered documentation that the United States government sup-pressed and destroyed crucial evidence disproving the necessity for evacuation on the grounds of military threat or necessity.

In November 1983, a federal court in San Francisco vacated Korematsu's original conviction. The presiding judge found no justification for the government-ordered internment. In 1984, a judge vacated Minoru Yasui's conviction, but refused to rule on the issue of governmental misconduct. Yasui appealed, but died in 1986, thereby mooting his appeal. In 1986, a federal district court in Seattle vacated Gordon Hirabayashi's 1942 conviction. [38]

The <u>coram nobis</u> cases, which received considerable media attention, provided momentum to the redress movement and, more importantly, proved that the gov-ernment had no legal basis for the evacuation and internment.

National Council for Japanese American Redress (NCJAR)

The NCJAR, led by Chicagoan William Hohri, believed that the most direct route to achieving redress existed in the judicial courts, as opposed to the JACL's legislative strategy. In 1983, the NCJAR filed a multibillion dollar class action suit in federal court on behalf of the one hundred and twenty thousand former internees. After sev-eral rulings and appeals, the United States Supreme Court in 1987 heard the case of the U.S. vs. Hohri et al. The Court, however, sent the case back to the federal Court of Appeals, which ruled in the government's favor. Prior to the case being heard again before the Supreme Court, President Reagan signed the Civil Liberties Act of 1988, thereby making judicial action moot. [39]

NCRR Lobbying Trip: Summer 1984

The Commission hearings and its subsequent report gave us confidence. In addition to our letter-writing efforts, NCRR decided to lobby Congressional representatives. Along with the JACL, NCRR members actively lobbied representatives at the local, state and national level. We sent letters to the President of the United States, members of Congress, and even their wives, to educate them and encourage their support for redress and reparations. From 1986 to 1988, we mailed over twenty-five thousand letters along with over six hundred mailgrams to Congress. I kept count of every letter mailed. They were like precious jewels to me.

Our first lobbying trip to Washington, D.C. took place in the summer of 1984. We spent three days in our nation's capitol and targeted about ten members of Congress. Our group included Marlene Tonai, Naomi Kubota, and me from the Bay Area NCRR; Bert Nakano, Miya Iwataki, and Kay Ochi from the Los Angeles NCRR; Tom Izu, Julie Hatta, and Gary Jio from the San Jose Nihonmachi Outreach Committee; and Bill Kochiyama, a community activist and former 442nd Regimental Combat Team veteran, joined us from New York. Jim Fukumoto, then an aide to Rep. Mervyn Dymally (D-California), arranged our meetings.

Without having had any previous lobbying experience, we gingerly knocked on Congressional doors the first morning and prayed that we would be welcomed. Feeling nervous and anxious, I half expected a big bear to come out of the door. I had to remind myself with each knock on the door that these representatives were our paid public servants and that we had every right to address them.

We remembered well that Commission member, Rep. Dan Lungren, had openly opposed the idea of monetary reparations, believing our country would never support it. We went to his office first because we wanted to let the Congressman know that we were disappointed with his decision. Lungren didn't meet with us; he sent an aide instead. Those of us who were former internees talked about the camps. I related how devastating Tanforan was, and how humiliating it felt living in a horsestall. My voice broke as I spoke about the awful food we ate. That meeting frustrated and saddened us because Mr. Lungren, related his aide, was adamant about his decision. The incident taught us, though, the value of taking risks. It made us thicker-skinned politically and stronger personally.

After we left Mr. Lungren's office, Naomi turned to me and asked, "Sox, why do you always cry when you talk about the food in camp?" I had to laugh at that, but that first meal sticks with me because it was such a degrading and devastating experience. There I stood in line in a mess hall, having someone dump food onto my plate when only an hour earlier I had been in Mrs. Perkin's dining room eating a nice breakfast and drinking out of fancy goblets. It was simply too much for me to take. That memory really hits me hard — that and being physically searched at the camp gate.

The trip was an incredible and productive learning experience. Many members that we lobbied sympathized with us and supported redress. Representative Dymally let us use his office as a work and storage space. As first-time lobbyists, we needed all the help we could get. He was wonderful to show us such generosity. We also fortunately met with Rep. Barney Frank (D-Massachusetts). He told us not to waste any time with him because he already supported redress. His words were a big boost for us. Encouragement like his gave us the courage to follow our convictions. And, later in the campaign, we followed his advice and focused our work on those members who clearly were against redress.

We continued our letter-writing efforts and public outreach. We sponsored workshops and rallies to educate our community and the public about the camps. In addition, we organized annual Day of Remembrance programs in various cities and locales, held on the anniversary of the signing of Executive Order 9066 [February 19, 1942], to raise public awareness.

Letters signed by people in the community played both a significant and symbolic role in the different phases of the redress movement. People believed that they made a difference by participating in the democratic process. The Issei at the Kimochi Nutrition Program would sign the letters with hands trembling, saying they knew the importance of letting the President and Congress members know that what was done to them was wrong. This was probably the first and only time that most of them had ever written such a letter.

Of the numerous areas that we canvassed in the Bay Area for signatures, I most enjoyed visiting the city of Berkeley. Going there always energized me. The residents I met were full of encouragement and highly informed about the internment. Over the course of two weekends, John Ota and I set up a letter-signing table in front of the popular Monterey Market in North Berkeley. Mr. William Fujimoto, the owner, was very accommodating, and we appreciated his show of support. We also were thankful for friends like Lucy Hamai and Sadie Sakamoto, Berkeley residents, who dropped by and brought us refreshments. That's grass-roots support at its best!

 Passersby approached us without any prompting and asked, "What would you like me to do?" They didn't hesitate to help us. What a refreshing change not to have to convince people of the injustice! A number of these individuals not only signed our letters but went into the market to find their spouses and friends to have them sign letters as well. Their friendly and understanding faces touched us, and we tried to thank every one of them.

I have one special memory regarding our letter-writing efforts. We had set up a letter-signing table at an Alameda Buddhist Temple bazaar. A young Caucasian girl, who couldn't have been more than eight or nine years old, passed by our table and looked at the donation can we had set out. She came hopping and skipping up to the table several more times, and each time went running back to her mother. She must've finally gathered up enough courage because she shyly approached the table, smiled, and dropped a quarter into the can and skipped away. I was genuinely moved by her gesture, especially in light of the fact that some Japanese Americans avoided our table like the plague.

Not everyone in our community supported the idea of redress and reparations; some openly resented our efforts. A few personal encounters left me shocked and upset. I remember several individuals stopping me on the streets of Japantown and reprimanding me. They insisted that NCRR shouldn't push for redress. What an insult, they argued, to think that money could remedy what happened during the war. "My father would turn over in his grave if I accepted any reparations," one gentleman sternly told me. His father's losses, he pointed out, were far too great to accept a token settlement of twenty thousand dollars. All I could say in return was that NCRR's intent wasn't solely monetary reparations but to fight for a basic principle. Our government had a responsibility to acknowledge its actions during the war, I said, and the consequences those actions had on our lives. The monetary compensation we sought would only make the apology more meaningful. He remained unconvinced.

A number of my good friends showed no interest in NCRR's efforts. I would sometimes wave and motion to them to come over to our table to sign letters, but they would only wave back, sometimes without a smile on their faces. Some simply shook their heads.

A girlfriend of mine once came up to me as I sat at a letter-writing table. "Sox," she asked, "are you still doing this stupid thing? We're not going to get any money, you know." I was stunned and disappointed to hear that from a friend. Obviously no one could guarantee that we'd succeed, but I replied, "How do you know unless you try? No one else will pursue this if we don't take a stand." She didn't sign a letter then but later changed her mind.

Others openly started berating us whenever we solicited letters. These people didn't believe Congress would ever pass a redress bill. That was frustrating to hear, especially coming from community people. We needed encouragement and support in this uphill battle. After episodes like that, I would go home thinking, "We have to push hard for this more than ever!"

In general, I think the Japanese American community's reaction to the early stages of the redress campaign was one of caution. Back in the late 1970s and early 1980s, a good many people in the community believed it was impossible to get Congress to address this issue, that it wasn't realistic, and that if and when a redress and reparations bill ever did pass, no Issei or Nisei would be alive to see it. I was skeptical myself, until I attended that NCRR community meeting in 1980 and realized that if the Sansei were willing to fight for this cause, why wasn't I?

Maybe my generation, the Nisei, is more reserved and cautious about what we do or say because of our experiences during the war. Much more so than the Issei and younger generations. Some Japanese Americans sat back and waited to see how the redress and reparations movement progressed before they committed themselves or got involved. The war had turned our whole lives upside down, inside and out, and to this day it remains difficult — if not impossible — for some to talk about their lives in the camps. We were raised not to question or challenge authority, to do as we were told. So it isn't too surprising that some former internees were too afraid to sign our letters, believing they would be put on a governmental blacklist or even sent to jail. I had to assure one hesitant letter-signer that we had a right to let our government know how we felt, and that if doing so was against the law, then I would go to jail in his place. Some of my friends, in trying to get their friends to sign letters, would point to me and say in all seriousness, "I know this lady. You can trust her."

Reintroduction of Redress Bill: 1985

A redress bill, nearly identical to H.R. 4110 but symbolically named H.R. 442 after the famed all-Japanese American combat team, was reintroduced in the House on January 3, 1985, this time with ninety-nine co-sponsors and Rep. Jim Wright again serving as lead sponsor. Sen. Spark Matsunaga introduced a redress bill in the Senate with twenty-five co-sponsors on May 2, 1985. Both bills died in this 99th Congress. H.R. 442 failed to make it to a vote, while the Senate bill, S. 1053, did not even get a hearing before a subcommittee. [40]

The Third Try: 1987

Critical changes occurred in 1987. More sympathetic redress supporters gained key leadership positions in the House and Senate of the 100th Congress. On January 6, 1987, Majority Leader Tom Foley (D-Washington), with one hundred and twenty-four co-sponsors, reintroduced H.R. 442. It passed out of the Judiciary Committee on June 17, 1987. Sen. Spark Matsunaga introduced the Senate bill, S. 1009, on April 10, 1987 with an amazing number of co-sponsors: over seventy, out of one hundred total Senators. [41]

Coalition Lobbying Trip: July 1987

I cannot emphasize enough the tenacious work of members of the JACL, NCRR, the 442nd Regimental Combat Team,[42] and others, who went to Washington, D.C. in the summer heat of July 1987, to lobby Congress.

There were nearly one hundred and thirty people who joined forces and lobbied along with our Japanese American members of Congress: Reps. Robert Matsui and Norman Mineta, and Sens. Daniel Inouye and Spark Matsunaga. These Congressmen had the political savvy to know when to wait and when to push forward on the issue. I couldn't participate in this trip. It was an extremely successful lobbying effort because the number of House co-sponsors climbed to over two hundred.

In August, the Senate Governmental Affairs Committee passed the redress bill unanimously. On September 17, 1987, fittingly the two hundredth anniversary of the signing of the Constitution, the House held a debate on H.R. 442 and finally gave its approval by a vote of 243-141. [43]

Over at the Japanese Cultural and Community Center of Northern California in San Francisco's Japantown, we waited intently to hear the vote count. When the final tally was recorded, we hugged and cried. Some even jumped up on the tables with joy. We had won one major battle!

Action progressed more slowly than expected in the Senate, which finally passed its redress bill, 69-27, on April 20, 1988. Both the House and Senate approved a final version of the bill in early August 1988. [44] *The biggest hurdle remained: Would President Reagan sign the bill, or would he veto it, as the U.S. Department of Justice had recommended?*

VII

A Witness to History

President Ronald Reagan had given no clear indication whether he would sign the Civil Liberties Act of 1988 after the bill cleared the House and Senate. The NCRR decided to launch a mailgram campaign to the President and members of Congress as a final push. Along the way, we hoped and prayed that President Reagan would sign the redress bill and correct a historical injustice.

We set up an account with Western Union, offering three message mailgrams from which to choose. Over six hundred people responded to this campaign and sent mailgrams at their own expense. That was fantastic. One evening I phoned in as many as twenty messages from different individuals and even got to know a few of the operators by name in the process.

The purposes of the Civil Liberties Act of 1988, P.L. 100-383, were as follows: 1) to acknowledge the fundamental injustice of the evacuation, relocation, and internment of U.S. citizens and permanent resident aliens of Japanese ancestry during World War II; 2) to apologize on behalf of the people of the United States for the evacuation, relocation, and internment of such citizens and permanent resident aliens; 3) to provide for a public education fund to finance efforts to inform the public about the internment of such individuals so as to prevent the recurrence of any similar event; 4) to make restitution [in the amount of twenty thousand dollars] to those individuals of Japanese ancestry who were interned and living at the time of the bill's enactment, August 10, 1988; 5) to make restitution [in the amount of twelve thousand dollars] to Aleut residents of the Pribilof Islands and the Aleutian Islands west of Unimak Island. [45]

The community rejoiced when President Reagan declared he would sign the bill![46] We received word on Monday evening, August 8, that the signing would take place on August 10, sometime between 11 a.m. and 2 p.m. The NCRR-San Francisco selected me and my best friend Katherine Nunotani to attend the ceremony as representatives. Even though we had no official invitation to attend, Katherine and I decided to make the historic trip to Washington, D.C. regardless. I pulled out the suitcase I had packed two months earlier in anticipation of the bill's passage. We left the next day.

It was unclear at first where the actual signing would take place or who would be attending. With sheer guts and fingers crossed, Katherine and I left for Washington, D.C. on August 9. We flew by the seat of our pants. We had no hotel reservations in D.C. upon leaving San Francisco, but we were determined to be present at the signing ceremony as NCRR members. Even if we didn't get in to the actual ceremony, we wanted to try to personally thank all the members of Congress who supported the bill.

We arrived at Dulles International Airport that evening, still without hotel reservations. We called fellow NCRR member John Ota in San Francisco, who was making the arrangements for us. We stood by a pay phone in the deserted airport, two old ladies waiting for John's return call. Katherine and I agreed that if we had to sleep on a bench right there at the airport, we were going to do just that. Then the phone rang. John had managed to secure a hotel room for us after all, and we settled in for the night.

The next morning, Wednesday, August 10, was a momentous day. We got up early to visit some of our Congressional supporters. The signing of the bill had been delayed until 2:30 p.m. so that gave us some more time.

Around lunch time, as we walked through the U.S. House building, we spotted Grayce Uyehara, the JACL-Legislative Education Committee executive director, at a doorway. She was greeting JACL members who had flown in for the ceremony from their national convention in Seattle. Grayce called out to us and invited us in. Representative Mineta was hosting a luncheon for them prior to the signing. I explained that we hadn't been invited, but she insisted we join in, saying that there were extra seats and that we shouldn't be bashful. Bert Nakano, NCRR's national spokesman from Los Angeles, was also in the building and invited to participate. I didn't think I had that kind of nerve to "crash" an event, but we accepted the invitation and joined the crowd.

JACL members and redress supporters from around the country filled the room and [then] JACL national president Cressey Nakagawa motioned to us to join him at his table. Katherine and I sat down; Bert spotted some friends at another table and sat with them.

Representative Mineta asked all of us to identify ourselves and our JACL affiliation. I was the first to say that I was a member of the National Coalition for Redress and Reparations. Many heads turned in my direction, perhaps in surprise. As a longtime member of the NCRR and the JACL, I'm equally honored to be involved with both.

Disagreements over who did what for redress and how much was done by individuals and groups such as the JACL, NCRR, and NCJAR have arisen and may always exist. My belief is that each person and group involved contributed in some way to the success of the overall movement. Some contributions received more attention or recognition than others, but every contribution was meaningful.

Afterwards, Norm (Mineta) came over to Katherine and me and asked for our Social Security numbers. He left the room and returned ten minutes later. He came over, gave me a hug, and shouted, "You're in!" We had received security clearance to attend the signing ceremony! Those two words made my whole day. I glanced over at Katherine and became very teary-eyed at the thought that as NCRR members, we were actually going to witness history in the making. I abruptly reached for my water glass to keep from crying.

As we waited outside of Room 450 of the Old Executive Office Building, where President Reagan was to sign the bill, I noticed a security woman roping off the area. She was allowing people in wheelchairs to enter first. We stood with Mary and Al Tsukamoto from Sacramento, California. The security guard signaled for the Tsukamotos to come forward and enter. She then signaled to Katherine and me to go in. I guess with my gray hair she figured I was too old to be standing around.

When we entered, the room was already buzzing with excitement. Many people toted video cameras. I found a seat, just three rows from the stage. Soon the room began quieting down as people took their seats. The President of the United States was introduced and at that moment I felt completely awed. "This is it!" I said to myself. I found myself thinking about all the work — the setbacks and successes — it took to make this day possible. We hadn't heard the President acknowledge the redress movement or the internment of Japanese Americans throughout our struggle, and we worried endlessly that he wouldn't come through. But here we were, about to see history made.

President Reagan read from a speech he made in 1945, in which Kazuo Masuda, a Japanese American veteran, posthumously received the Distinguished Service Cross medal for his valor during World War II.[47] The speech read, in part, "Blood that has soaked into the sands of a beach is all of one color. America stands unique in the world, the only country not founded on race, but on a way, an ideal." He leaned over the stage and shook hands with June Masuda Goto, Kazuo's sister.

I can actually say that I saw President Reagan put his signature to the bill. It was such an emotional moment. I wept with others around me and experienced a flood of relief. I can't remember how, but I got onto the stage to thank

Representatives Mineta and Matsui. As the three of us hugged each other, no one said a word. Feelings ran high throughout the room as men and women openly cried.

Right after the signing, I ran out into the hallway, looking for a telephone to call friends over the Japanese Cultural and Community Center of Northern California,[48] and Kimochi in San Francisco.[49] The community was on cloud nine and ready to burst. A festive celebration took place at the cultural center. I tried to picture my friends' reactions to the news back home and felt so elated. I slept well that night. I couldn't wait to get home.

I do regret, and feel saddened, that Representative Dymally, an early and ardent supporter of redress, had been overlooked at the bill's signing. I don't think he had been invited. The following day a group of us went to his office to express our apologies. He should've been there with us. He exhibited nothing but graciousness toward us.

On the plane ride back to San Francisco, I reflected on the past years. I hoped we had now made believers out of the skeptics and doubters. I thought about how fortunate I was to have attended the first community redress meeting and testified before the Commission, which involved me closely with the Sansei. Had it not been for the redress movement, I probably wouldn't have had much contact with people so much younger than myself. And that would've meant missing out on the opportunity to know, and work with, such wonderful individuals. Even though I'm twice as old as most of the Sansei in NCRR, they always treated me like one of them. I'm extremely proud of this third generation of Japanese Americans.

I also wondered whether I would've been able to involve myself as much as I had in the redress effort had Tom still been alive. It has required a lot of my time and energy. I'd like to think that we would've been involved together.

VIII

Breaking New Ground

Office of Redress Administration (ORA)

After President Reagan signed the Civil Liberties Act of 1988, the Office of Redress Administration (ORA) in the Civil Rights Division of the Department of Justice opened in September 1988. Charged with implementing provisions of the bill, the ORA set out to identify and verify individuals potentially eligible for monetary redress.

Individuals eligible for redress had to fulfill the following requirements: be of Japanese ancestry;[50] a U.S. citizen or permanent resident alien at the time of the internment period — December 7, 1941 to June 30, 1946; and living on the date of the bill's enactment, August 10, 1988. After verifying an individual's eligibility, the ORA then sent letters and forms requesting additional information and documents to establish one's identity. If an individual had died since the enactment of the law on August 10, 1988, payment would then pass on to a spouse, children, or parents, in that order. If no survivor(s) existed, the money reverted to the Civil Liberties Public Education Fund.

The ORA obtained historic records, primarily from the National Archives in Washington, D.C., and updated information from federal and state government agencies to verify potential eligibles. As the Act intended, the oldest eligible individuals received their payments first; the last group to be paid would be those born in the camps. In determining preliminary eligibility for redress, thousands of individuals provided historical information by filing out voluntary information forms.

As a contact person for the NCRR in San Francisco, I volunteered to help people with their applications. I began receiving countless calls from Japanese Americans after the bill's signing. Calls came not only from the local area and throughout California, but from such places as Hawai`i, Illinois, Washington, D.C., Idaho, Washington state, New Mexico, New York, Utah, Florida, Louisiana, and even Japan.

I'm amazed at how total strangers would call and share their very personal experiences with me. That's a bond we former internees share. I heard unique stories and learned interesting historical facts. Some veterans related to me how, in 1943, at Fort Riley, Kansas, where the 442nd RCT trained, President Franklin D. Roosevelt inspected the Army camps for morale purposes. The Japanese American soldiers, however, were rounded up and locked in the motor pool warehouse to keep them out of sight. Hearing stories like that depressed me.

Occasionally people related humorous accounts about particular events or situations. For the most part, though, I listened to stories of real trauma and tragedy. Yet even at that, people hesitated to apply for reparations. Their resistance only made me feel more motivated and determined. I wanted every single person who was entitled to redress to apply!

Since the redress program had no precedent, changes and adjustments to the application process seemed inevitable. At first the redress office required notarized copies of all documents submitted to them. The time and cost involved in doing this was hard on the Issei — the first group of recipients — especially if they had no means of transportation or lived on a fixed income. In San Francisco we were truly fortunate that T. Okamoto and Co., a longtime insurance and realty business in Japantown, provided this service free of charge. To our collective relief, the redress office later eliminated this requirement.

To help disseminate information and provide assistance, the ORA began sending personnel from its Washington, D.C. office to conduct informational workshops in various cities with sizable Japanese American populations — Los Angeles, San Francisco, San Jose, Seattle, for example. ORA Administrator Robert (Bob) K.

Bratt, his deputy Paul Suddes, and other staff members usually led the sessions. In San Francisco alone, hundreds of people turned out.

During the first phase of the program, which focused on the oldest eligible survivors, I derived great pleasure working with the Issei. I did most of my one-on-one work with them at the Kimochi lunch site and was amazed to find that a number of them had kept complete historical documents from the war years. At one of the San Francisco workshops, an Issei woman unwrapped a pass she had been issued back in 1942 to evacuate voluntarily. Clearly, she safeguarded this card because it looked brand new, as though it had just been issued. She didn't seem to realize the importance of having the card until I explained to her that without such documentation, voluntary evacuees had difficulty proving they relocated.

On occasion I made home visits to those unable to come to Japantown. I remember paying a visit to a lady who called me at the Kimochi office, quite eager for us to meet. I went to her home. Upon my arrival, she practically yanked me from the door into her kitchen to tell me she was convinced that her children had cashed her twenty thousand dollar redress check, because, as "evidence," she had seen them with new furniture. I couldn't help myself, so I chuckled and said, "But, *obasan* (an affectionate Japanese term for "aunt"), no money has been paid to anyone yet." She was embarrassed but equally relieved to hear that.

Once the redress office approved an application for redress, many Issei understandably became anxious. They'd say things like, "Can you hurry up the process? I'm eighty-nine years old and I want to live long enough to hear the President's apology." It was hard to know what to say to them since we had no idea how much longer they'd have to wait. All I could say was, *"Ganbatte, ne?"* (please persevere; hang on).

IX

Potholes in the Road

"The story of redressing Japanese Americans for their wartime loss of constitutional rights did not end with the bill's passage on August 10, 1988; the President's signature marked one major high point in a long and complicated trail of peaks and valleys. The effort to secure the necessary funds to pay eligible internees, many of whom were quite elderly, before they died was nearly as much of an ordeal as getting H.R. 442 [The Civil Liberties Act of 1988] passed in the first place." [51]

Five months after he signed H.R. 442, President Ronald Reagan absolutely disappointed and insulted us by not proposing any redress funds for fiscal year 1989, and only twenty million dollars for fiscal year 1990.

NCRR Lobbying Trip: August 10-14, 1989

In August 1989, members of the NCRR [52] traveled again to Washington, D.C. — our third lobbying trip — to push for an increase in the twenty million dollar appropriation proposed by President Reagan. We felt a sense of urgency over this issue because former internees were only growing older or passing away. [53]

Since this was, in all likelihood, our final lobbying trip to D.C. — or so we hoped if Congress and the President approved a higher appropriation — we wanted to do something visual and symbolic. So we decided to bring thousands of colorful Japanese paper *(origami)* cranes [54] to present to members of Congress and Department of Justice officials. The cranes, we explained to people, represented "love and peace." Several generations of Japanese

Americans and others, from Issei women at the Kimochi lounge in San Francisco to some of Brent Mori's fellow students at UC Berkeley, had folded them. I always laugh in remembering how Brent, a young activist and NCRR member, traveled all the way to Washington with a suitcase filled with paper birds.

Kathryn Korematsu, Katherine Nunotani, Miya Iwataki, Dorothy Kojima, Brent and I sewed the cranes together and attached them to wooden dowels that we presented to each congressional member we visited. We also presented cranes to U.S. Deputy Assistant Attorney General James Turner. People took notice as we walked around the halls of Congress with these colorful birds in hand. They marveled at the cranes and asked their significance. It was a good entree to talk about what happened to Japanese Americans during the war. Brent, showing his resourcefulness, actually packed lumber, a hammer, saw, nails, needle and thread, and constructed a stand on which we draped the cranes. Not only was he a university student, but he became a carpenter as well on this trip. He showed a lot of fight and commitment.

We targeted primarily Senate offices, since a budget hearing on redress was imminent. We visited Sen. Ernest Hollings' (D-South Carolina) office because he was chair of the subcommittee allocating money for redress. While he didn't support redress, he said he wouldn't express his opposition. We also paid a visit to Sen. Alan Cranston (D-California), who was rather unreceptive to us. We had scheduled an appointment with him, but, even then, it took a while before we could get in to see him. When he finally came out to meet us, he didn't invite us into his office. He stood in the doorway of his office and talked to us out in the hall. We weren't pleased about that visit.

Brent, whose father Floyd was a former California legislator, met with Sen. Pete Wilson (R-California). Sen. Paul Simon (D-Illinois) was very supportive and talked with us along with his aide. We were fortunate to see Sen. Spark Matsunaga (D-Hawai`i) on this trip. He invited us in and served us refreshments. He appeared frail but still had that fighting spirit and gave us a ton of encouragement. We went on to visit the offices of Sen. Daniel Inouye (D-Hawai`i), Sen. Richard Gephardt (D-Missouri), Sen. Phil Gramm (R-Texas), Sen. Jim Sasser (D-Tennessee), Sen. Mark Hatfield (R-Oregon), and Sen. Warren Rudman (R-New Hampshire).

We paid a courtesy call to Representative Dymally and again thanked him for his support and assistance over the years. He was most helpful to our cause. Of course, we also met with Representatives Matsui and Mineta, two people who continually kept our spirits up. They worked ceaselessly to see justice prevail. Representative Matsui held a reception for us, which we really appreciated. Throughout the course of the trip, it was heart-warming to hear other Congressional representatives heap praise on their Japanese American colleagues.

We participated in a redress appropriations press conference, which was held on the steps of the Capitol. Various media came to cover our event, and it went well. We displayed the paper cranes at the top of the steps, and I spoke on behalf of the NCRR. Fred Korematsu, one of three individuals who challenged the constitutionality of the wartime evacuation orders back in the 1940s, and who was subsequently arrested, convicted and jailed, talked about his experiences during and after the war.

On this trip we learned that Senators Inouye and Matsunaga were working on establishing redress as an entitlement program. An entitlement meant that the redress program wouldn't have to compete year after year for precious funding against other domestic programs, foreign aid, military spending, and the like, because the funding would be guaranteed.[55] Appropriations for these programs are automatically set aside. We felt if redress became an entitlement, that would be nothing short of a miracle.

One evening during the trip, we held a summit meeting in one of the hotel rooms. We went around the room to get people's opinions about the trip. Some of the younger people had tears in their eyes as they spoke, saying they had learned a great deal, especially about the political process. Brent felt he learned something of value from the trip. I found it heartwarming to see the future of our community in these young activists.

A senate budget committee hearing on redress had been scheduled for the following day. Because the room had limited seating, Katherine (Nunotani) and I arose early and lined up outside the room with others. Luckily, we just made it in. Katherine brought with her a string of cranes, which she taped to the wall of the hearing room. Sen. Ernest Hollings immediately instructed her to take it down. The hearing had already begun.

Redress became an entitlement program, thanks largely to Senator Inouye. President Bush signed the appropriations bill on November 21, 1989. After a decade of ups and downs, and four decades since the birth of the internment camps, the government was *finally* going to apologize for its actions and begin paying reparations.

My daily work in helping people with their applications continued and really picked up once it was certain that money would be available to start individual payments to former internees and evacuees.

Redress and Art

In 1990, there were two "firsts" for me; both were related to my work on redress. Bay Area jazz musician Jon Jang asked me to emcee the ninth annual Asian American Jazz Festival at the Asian Art Museum in Golden Gate Park. Held on March 3, 1990, this entertaining and original event showcased Asian American talent.

While I felt honored to be asked, I hesitated because I had never done anything like it before. Jon, the leader, pianist and composer of the Pan Asian Arkestra, was a longtime supporter of redress and a good friend. He encouraged me to do it. The intent of this particular festival, he said, was to pay tribute to the redress movement and celebrate the fact that redress payments would begin in the fall. I accepted. I thoroughly enjoyed myself despite being nervous throughout the evening.

In 1990 Jon also released an album, entitled *Never Give Up!* on which he included one of my Day of Remembrance speeches. We had recorded "Let Us Not Forget" in its entirety back in September 1989 for this album, which he dedicated to the redress movement.[56] A *taiko* (a big drum) and bass play in the background as I recite my speech. I was happy to participate in this project; it was an exciting experience I'll not soon forget. I had had no idea how much was involved in a professional recording, and I certainly have a greater appreciation for it all.

X

A Wish Come True

A long awaited dream became reality on the morning of October 9, 1990. The nine oldest living former internees received the first redress checks at the Great Hall of Justice in Washington, D.C.

Bob Bratt of the ORA invited me to the presentation ceremony. I was overjoyed about going. The trip was made even more special because just before I left San Francisco, I learned that a newly hired Kimochi employee, Yumi Yuge, was the granddaughter of one of the nine recipients. I invited Yumi to go with me to Washington. I spoke to her supervisor about it, and she gave Yumi time off to attend this once-in-a-lifetime event.

After arriving in D.C., Yumi and I were part of the contingent on hand to greet some of the recipients at Dulles International Airport. They were excited! Yumi's grandfather, Senkichi Yuge, was 101 years of age and lived in Los Angeles. He had fainted the night before; Yumi made calls throughout the night to get updates on his condition. "I hope he can attend," I said to Yumi. "This is an historical event." She replied, "Even if it is the last thing he does, he will make it." Yumi's grandfather's family and friends in Los Angeles encouraged him to make this trip and become a part of history, even though he was slightly weak. Yumi's mother accompanied him.

From the beginning of my involvement with the redress and reparations movement, my private wish was to shake the hand of the oldest recipient, who turned out to be a one hundred and eight-year-old gentleman from Phoenix, Arizona. He suffered from an ailment, however, and was unable to attend the ceremony. The ORA had contacted the next oldest living recipient, Rev. Mamoru Eto, a one hundred and seven-year-old from Los Angeles. I met Reverend Eto at the airport. He was ecstatic to be in Washington, D.C. He kept taking his gloves off and raising seven fingers to indicate that he was one hundred and seven years old. His son, who accompanied him, said his father was forever telling people how old he was. I laughed and said, "Well, if you live to be one hundred and seven, you're certainly entitled to."

Paul Suddes, deputy administrator of the ORA, rented a van to transport the recipients to a hotel in Georgetown. I went with them. Paul and Frank Pfeiffer, a senior researcher at the ORA, escorted them to their rooms and helped them settle in. One of the recipient's flights, however, was delayed for more than an hour, which meant one more run to the airport. By the time the last of the group arrived, it was late. Thankfully, everyone arrived safely.

Before I left the hotel at 11 p.m., I overheard Paul say to Frank, "Let's go check on each one once more before I leave." Frank, who speaks Japanese, stayed with the recipients at the hotel to ensure that everyone was taken care of. Paul and Frank scurried around like mother hens. They were conscientious and caring, and it was touching to watch them in action. I was happy that Yumi was able to spend some time with her mother and grandfather. Her grandfather died only two months later.

On the morning of October 9, members of Congress, family members of the nine recipients, news media, ORA employees, members of the Justice Department, and Japanese Americans from all over the country filled the Great Hall. Cameras and lights were everywhere; media from throughout the country, as well as Japan and Europe, were on hand. What a grand day it was!

Before the presentation began, I spotted Bob seated near the stage. I went up to say hello. He looked exhausted, and I blurted out, "Bob, you look so old!" He turned to me and cracked, "Thanks, Sox. What a way to greet a person!" I felt bad for saying that, but he *did* look exhausted, a result of all the work and effort he put in as the ORA administrator, and in making sure everything was in place for this day.

Several members of Congress — Senator and Mrs. Daniel Inouye, among them — sat directly in front of me. I scanned this row of powerful members of Congress who helped pave the way to victory. How fortunate we were to have these highly respected Congressmen. Without their help we couldn't have realized redress and reparations. People like Representatives Mineta and Matsui gave us hope and the strength to persevere. I wanted so much to thank each one of these members for their integrity and inspiration and to tell them the obvious: that what we were about to see was the result of their unwavering efforts, their support, and encouragement.

Fittingly, Reverend Eto gave the invocation. Attorney General Richard Thornburgh knelt beside each recipient to present a twenty thousand dollar check along with the letter of apology from President George Bush. He said, "I'm sorry it took so long." The room was heavy with emotion. Bob remarked that for those who wondered if redress would ever happen, "It just did." It was a golden moment for these nine oldest survivors.

One hundred-year-old Sugi Kiriyama of California bowed her head and prayed after she received her check from Attorney General Thornburgh. Her granddaughter related to reporters, "She's been praying everyday that she would still be alive [for this]." Sada Ide of Virginia was ninety years old, one of the "younger" beneficiaries. She had waited for this day for a long time, "waiting, waiting, waiting," she told reporters. When asked what she would do with her money, Ide replied, "I'm going to buy a house and have my own garden."

The other initial recipients were: Haru Dairiki (102) from California; Kisa Iseri (102) from Oregon; Hisano Fujimoto (101) from Illinois; Don Hatsuki Shima (86) and Ken Yamamoto (73) both from Maryland.

In his address, Attorney General Thornburgh said, in part, *"We enjoy a precious system of government that is unsurpassed by any in the world. Even when that system failed you, you never lost your faith in it. On the contrary, you believed that through that system you could achieve the justice which you had been denied. By finally admitting a wrong, a nation does not destroy its integrity but, rather, reinforces the sincerity of its commitment to the Constitution and hence, to its people. In forcing us to reexamine our history, you have made us only stronger and more proud."*

That evening, the Fox Network contacted me at my hotel and asked me to appear on a live show the next morning. I hesitated but finally agreed to do it. They sent a cab for me at around 7 a.m. It seemed like we drove forever, to the point that I became a little wary of the riding so far with a perfect stranger. The driver must've sensed my anxiety as he turned to me and told me to relax. To my relief we finally reached the studio. It turned out I was the only guest on the show. The interviewer asked questions about the internment and listened to my personal reflections. If just one viewer learned something about the camps, it was well worth it.

How perfect it would've been if every Issei and former internee had been there to witness the check presentation. It was a bittersweet achievement. Our community had come far in this struggle. Cohesion was sometimes difficult to come by, especially in the early stages, but, on this day, the spirit of our community prevailed. We had met tremendous opposition and budget disappointments, but we didn't allow ourselves to give up. For the NCRR, it had meant ten long years to ensure that future generations would never again have their constitutional rights abrogated. We would not let America forget.

San Francisco Ceremony

One week later, at the Hinode Towers in San Francisco Japantown, a residential facility for the elderly, John Dunne, U.S. Assistant Attorney General for the Civil Rights Division, presented redress checks to five women and one man. Bob flew in for this and was the main speaker. Hundreds of people turned out for this event. Tears flowed freely.

The six recipients were: Kiyoshi Yamashita (95); Mitsu Sato (101); Chiyo Mizuno (100); Mary Chiyo Okinaga (95); Tokiyo Iwamoto (95); and Kiyo Fukayama (94), who told reporters she intended to give her money to the local senior center and to her four-and-a-half-month-old grandson toward his education.

Civil rights attorney Dale Minami of San Francisco, who was the lead attorney for Fred Korematsu in the historic *coram nobis* cases, opened the program by reflecting, *"Forty-eight years after the imprisonment of Japanese Americans, and almost twenty years after the redress struggle began, we have received some vindication. But we will experience this day of triumph with a sense of sadness, sobered by the memory of sixty-five thousand former internees who are no longer with us today. It is in honor of their memory that we dedicate this celebration."*

Dale and other speakers praised Bob for his compassion and sensitivity as the administrator of the redress program. They presented him with a *daruma*[57] doll and asked him to fill in the missing eye of the doll, which he did to the cheers of onlookers. The audience observed a moment of silence for the late Sen. Spark Matsunaga,[58] a beloved and long-standing member of Congress, for his tremendous and untiring determination to see redress come to fruition.

XI

One-On-One

First Payment Period: October, 1990

In the beginning of the redress program, more than a few Japanese Americans felt both *enryo* (a Japanese expression, loosely translated, meaning to hold back, to feel reserved or be modest) about applying for redress, and *haji* (a Japanese term meaning shame, disgrace, dishonor) for accepting money for all that we went through. After the first redress checks were presented, however, attitudes changed, and disbelievers became believers. The Presidential apology was meaningful, and some people truly needed the money. There was no shame in that. I was elated as gradually more people began asking for applications.

Confusion continued in our community about how the payment process worked. Many people became upset upon learning they hadn't yet applied for redress, believing that the early verification notice they received from the National Archives sufficed. We had to patiently explain that in addition to receiving archival information, individuals still had to actually apply for reparations. Confusion also surrounded the status of veterans, a good number of whom mistakenly believed they were ineligible for redress. It took some time before information got out that they could certainly apply for redress. Getting the correct information out to the community was much more difficult than we'd anticipated.

I did the majority of my work with people on an individual basis, helping them prepare applications or obtain verifications.

Just as every person is unique, so too is each case. I often found my interactions with men — husbands in particular — pretty humorous. Several husbands came to the redress workshops at their wives insistence. They came begrudgingly, thinking it a waste of time. To their surprise, they found their applications incomplete, and quietly remarked to me how glad they felt that their wives had "forced" them to attend. I'm sure they never admitted that to their wives.

During one of the ORA workshops in San Francisco, my friend Shig Doi and his wife Yoshiko were having a group of their 442nd friends over to their house. They did this about twice a year. As a 442nd veteran, Shig is active with the group. They asked me to come over, and I asked if I could invite Paul Suddes along so that he could explain the veterans' application process. Paul agreed to come, and the veterans seemed to appreciate his willingness to spend a day with them. Bob and Paul were terrific representatives of the ORA.

One gentleman who called me during the first payment period declared that he wasn't going to fill out a voluntary information form. He was quite bitter. "It's nice that you are helping people," he said, "but since the government put me in camp, let them do the legwork and find me." I said, "That is your choice, but I hope you'll think it over. It may take some time before the ORA can find current information on you. By the time they find you — if they do — you may have to wait a long time to get your money." I think I turned him around. He phoned me a few weeks later and asked for a form. I recognized his voice and am glad he reconsidered.

One eligible redress recipient was anxious to get her redress check. She told me she sat near her front door everyday waiting for the mailman to come. I tried to ease her mind, suggesting that she call me as soon as she received the check because I would then go with her to the bank to deposit it. One day she called to tell me she received it. She was so happy that she wept over the phone. Then I learned she was eager to get the money so that she could distribute it among her grandchildren. She, like many others, wanted the money only so that they could give it away.

An Issei woman asked me about the status of her case every time I saw her on the streets of Japantown or at community events, which was fairly often. On one occasion I phoned the redress office about her application and was told it was still being processed. The next time I called, I learned that her check had already been mailed some time ago. I quickly phoned this woman and asked if she remembered receiving a large brown envelope in the mail. She thought for a moment and then said, "Yes, I think so. I remember the word 'Washington' in the return address." I practically shouted, "*Obasan*, that must be it! You must already have it." She laughed and said, "I thought it was an advertisement and so I put it away in a drawer. I was planning to give it to my daughter the next time she comes to visit." She checked in the drawer, took out the envelope, and discovered her redress check was indeed inside. She laughed as she said to me, "This is what happens when you get old."

A sweet, compassionate Issei woman, who had no family, asked for my advice. She was torn about what to do with her redress money. She told me about an orphaned teenaged boy, a Japanese American, whom she had befriended before the war. When the evacuation order came, she offered to look after him since he had no family, and so they entered the camp together. They became like mother and son. When this young man turned nineteen years old, he volunteered for military service from the camp.

On this woman's eighty-first birthday, her "son" threw her a surprise party. His thoughtfulness touched her. She wanted to know what I thought about her officially adopting this man and giving him the redress money. If that was her wish, I told her, I would be happy to arrange legal help for her.

Early the next morning she came to see me and said she hadn't slept a wink. She had tossed the idea around in her head all night. She had decided not to adopt this man because she didn't want to put him in a position where he'd feel obligated to care for her if she ever became ill. I know of many Issei who don't want to burden others, and I admired her for it. Instead I suggested setting up a will. I referred her to an attorney at the Nihonmachi Legal Outreach[59] in Japantown. I don't know whether she ever did pursue it, but she seemed much more at ease with that option.

Second Payment Period: October 1991

The second group of redress recipients consisted mainly of the Nisei. This was the largest group I worked with. Complicated cases arose during this period. Most had a happy ending, but some did not.

One common problem was basic: getting an applicant's name right. When people got married in camps, their names changed and, as a result, differed from the archival records. Others changed their Japanese given names to American names or took on nicknames, which was quite popular among Nisei. That caused immense confusion. Names were also sometimes misspelled on birth certificates. Occasionally a quick call or a letter to the ORA straightened things out.

Other complications involved misinterpretations. If you were denied access to your property during the war — and this was especially applicable for veterans — you were eligible for redress. Many Japanese Americans, however, interpreted the word "property" to mean actual land or real estate, which wasn't necessarily true. As a result, some Japanese Americans didn't even bother applying. The definition of "property" could include personal items — clothing, books, for example — which couldn't be safeguarded during the war.

During the course of her work helping individuals with their redress applications, Sox came across a multitude of complicated and unusual cases. Determined to find answers and resolution for these people, most of them strangers, Sox spared no expense in her pursuit of the truth.

Thankfully Lady Luck smiled upon some of the cases I handled. One of the more unusual cases involved finding a homeless man in San Francisco. It was fall 1991, and the ORA asked me to locate and assist this man with his redress application.

This gentleman had submitted an application for redress but hadn't been in contact with the ORA for months. They needed an address and affidavits in order to complete his application. I didn't recognize this man's name at all, but when I mentioned it in passing to my son, he said knew who this person was and in fact had seen him before. A stroke of luck! He remembered this man because he had once hauled away an old refrigerator of ours.

The last known address for this individual, which the ORA furnished, turned out to be a confectionery store in San Francisco. I immediately went there and checked with the proprietor, who told me the man in question had no home and had used the store's address for correspondence purposes since he frequented the place. I decided I had nothing to lose, so I asked around in the store if anyone knew this gentleman. It just so happened that two people knew him! Right then and there on the spot, I asked them to verify some facts, which they did. About an hour later, I faxed all this information to the ORA from Japantown. They later informed me that the man, who lives out of a truck, received his redress check shortly thereafter.

I worked on the case of a young man whose application for redress was denied, even though his father and sister received their redress money. The family had been interned in Crystal City, Texas, a separate Justice Department camp for non-citizens. This man's father was interned there and his family joined him later.

We had been trying to find evidence to prove his internment but had reached a dead end. I happened to see this man at a National Japanese American Historical Society[60] event. During our conversation, he casually mentioned that his name once appeared in a book about Japanese Peruvians entitled, *Pawns in a Triangle of Hate: Japanese Peruvians and the United States*. He hadn't shared this information before. I practically screamed and said, "It is?" I told him to make a copy of the passage and send it to me right away. I then faxed this new information to the ORA. Coincidentally, it turned out that the ORA's special verification office had a copy of the book in its possession. Published in 1981, this important book has extensive documentation about the little known history of Peruvian Japanese who were interned in the United States. The book proved that this man was indeed detained in Crystal City, Texas. About a month later, I again ran into this man at a function in San Francisco. He showed me a copy of the form he received which declared him eligible for redress. He subsequently received his redress check.

At another community gathering, I learned about a young man who spent the war in a sanitarium. His sister mentioned the difficulty he was having in trying to prove his eligibility. I began working on his behalf. Individuals in these circumstances weren't allowed to evacuate with other Japanese Americans because of their condition. It was an involved case because the hospital in which this man was admitted as a patient no longer existed. I checked with county offices but learned that all records from that era had been destroyed. I finally turned to the U.S. Justice Department for help and found, surprisingly, that the government maintained records on these individuals, and, in fact, kept records of hospitals and institutions with Japanese American patients during the war. The day this man received his check was a joyous one for me.

Sox worked on several cases that illuminated the diversity and humanism of the Japanese American community. She became the lone advocate for destitute and disenfranchised individuals.

One of my cases which sadly went unresolved involved a Japanese American veteran. I find it hard to forget him.

On March 18, 1992, Harry Tanabe, a national officer with the Veterans of Foreign Wars (VFW), his wife Shiz, Wally

Nunotani, Commander of the Golden Gate Nisei Memorial Post 9879, and I, traveled to the Veterans' Home in Yountville, California, to visit perhaps the only Japanese American veteran who had resided there since June, 1979. His name was Tom.

We had learned about Tom through a friend of a friend. He was a shy man, a loner, who apparently had had no visitors in all the years he lived at the Home. Everyday, Tom walked around the grounds, carrying a brown paper bag and picking up trash with two twigs, which he wielded like chopsticks. He did this practically all day long.

Tom was probably entitled to redress our friend said and, in all likelihood, didn't know anything about it. Our friend asked if we would pay him a visit and see if he wanted to apply. We readily agreed.

After arriving at the Home and checking the grounds for Tom with no success, we located him in the cafeteria, where he was having his lunch. We didn't want to frighten or overwhelm him all at once, so we waited in the rear of the cafeteria while Harry went over and introduced himself. He explained who he was and offered Tom the services of the VFW. Harry then eased into the subject of redress and reparations and explained to Tom that he may be entitled to it. He gestured over to me and said that I could help with his application if he wanted. Tom hadn't heard about redress and reparations and was surprised such a thing existed. He said he wanted to apply, so I sat down with him to fill out an application form.

When I asked him for personal information, such as his Social Security number and veteran's identification number, he quickly pulled from out of his pants pocket a stack of cards bound with an old, discolored rubber band. You could tell he hadn't looked at those cards in a long time, but they were important enough that he kept them with him at all times. As he tried to undo the band, it suddenly crumbled like a potato chip. He didn't know what to do. I felt bad and rummaged through my purse, finding another rubber band which I handed to him. He found his veteran's card in the pile. Slowly I engaged him in conversation and found out that he originally came from Los Angeles. As we spoke further, it became apparent that Tom needed affidavits from people who knew him and who could attest to certain facts.

Before leaving the Home that afternoon, we asked to see the hospital administrator. We needed more information on Tom's background. To ensure that he, and not someone else, would get the redress money, we needed to find out whether or not he had a conservatorship or a power of attorney. Tom was unsure of this himself. The receptionist told us to have a seat, saying that the administrator would see us. As we sat there and waited, I sensed the office workers scrutinizing us and felt uneasy. I had even caught one of the clerks, an older Caucasian woman, peaking at us from between some binders on the counter. After waiting a long time, though, the receptionist told us he was busy and couldn't meet. We left the Home with more questions than answers.

Upon returning home, I turned to the local media for help. I explained the situation to Takeshi Nakayama, a reporter with the *Rafu Shimpo*, a Japanese American newspaper in Los Angeles. I needed to find people who knew Tom and who were willing to sign affidavits. Takeshi suggested I place an ad in the *Rafu*, requesting that anyone who might know Tom should contact me. We gave no reasons or explanations in the ad for wanting this information.

Within two days, I received a call from George O., a gentleman in Monterey Park in Southern California, informing me that Tom might in fact be his cousin. George explained that Tom had lived with his family for years even though they weren't blood relatives. Their families knew one another because George's mother and Tom's mother both came from the same village in Japan. Tom had lived with George's family since a fairly young age, so George considered him family. He asked if he could join us on our next visit to the veterans' home because he had lost track of Tom years ago.

We made our second trip to Yountville on June 4, 1992. George came up from Los Angeles and joined me, along with Diane Matsuda, a lawyer with Nihonmachi Legal Outreach in San Francisco, Wally Nunotani, and his daughter Karen Kern. At first we didn't know what to make of it when George repeatedly asked Tom, "Do you remember me?" and Tom replied, "No, I don't." George began naming members of his family, his sister, for example, and Tom responded, saying the names sounded familiar to him. Gradually he remembered more of George's family. George gave him an update on everyone and broke the news that his mother, Tom's surrogate mother, had died. Before her death, however, she had wanted to tell Tom that when his own time came, he was welcome to be buried in their family plot.

Diane spoke with Tom and tried to get answers about whether he had a power of attorney. He still couldn't remember but added that he didn't receive any of his Social Security and pension checks. That revelation made us even more concerned about his legal and financial status. Diane recommended to Tom that he consider drawing up a will.

It may well be that in the thirteen years he lived at the Home, Tom hadn't spoken as much as he did with us during the two trips we made to see him. When he spoke his voice was barely more than a whisper. Sadly he didn't seem to have any friends at the Home.

I briefly discussed with him what he wanted to do with the redress money should he receive it. He seemed at a loss. How about taking a trip somewhere, or trying to locate your long lost friends, I suggested. He insisted he didn't have any friends. He then piped up and said, "After I get the check, I'll just cash it and keep the money in my pocket." "Oh, you shouldn't do that," I cried out. "It's not safe." He seemed so innocent. He thought about it some more and said he wanted to give his money to a Southern California Buddhist church, where he had spent some time in his youth.

After our visit, Diane wrote to the VA administrator again (her previous letter had gone unanswered), requesting information regarding the existence of a conservator or whether receiving the twenty thousand dollars in redress money would have a detrimental effect on Tom's continued eligibility at the Home. We waited, feeling exasperated. Approximately three weeks later, we finally received a brief letter from the administrator stating that the VA couldn't provide us with any personal information. None of our questions were answered, and we were back to square one.

And then, in a shock to all of us, a few weeks later we learned that Tom had passed away. The news stunned us because he seemed to have been in good health. I felt terrible for a long time afterwards. His case went unresolved, and we could take no further action. I wish that I had had the power to investigate this case further. He was the first potential recipient who passed away before I was able to find resolution to his case.

George told us later that as a child Tom had been abused by his biological father. His mother had passed away when he was a mere youngster, so he grew up never knowing her. Evidently his father had simply abandoned him at a young age, leaving him in the care of George's family. It was heartbreaking to hear this and to realize that Tom had not only spent his latter years alone but had ultimately died alone, too.

In the early part of 1993, I received a startling call from the redress office to locate a Japanese American woman in San Francisco. This was another case which ended sadly.

An ORA contact phoned me one afternoon at home to ask whether a San Francisco address they had on file was anywhere near my apartment. It wasn't too far away, I replied. I was told that a woman had just called the ORA office but hung up abruptly because she said she was having trouble breathing. Concerned about her, the ORA gave me her name, address, and a phone number and asked if I'd go over. "I'll go and check on her right away," I said.

Since I don't drive, I telephoned my friend Karen Kern, who works down the street from where I live, for a lift. We walked up and down the street looking for the address I was given, with no luck. I flagged down a mailman and asked if he recognized the woman's name. He didn't. We drove to Karen's mother's house, which was nearby, to use the phone to call this woman. The phone rang several times with no answer. I called the ORA back to double check the number, but the office had already closed. I then called the phone company to verify this woman's telephone number and ran into another obstacle: she had an unlisted number and the operator couldn't release any information. I pleaded, explaining that this was a possible emergency, to which the operator said, "Then call the local police." I did.

The police told me they couldn't help and suggested I call "911" instead. I became increasingly frustrated by the minute. Before calling the emergency number, I took a chance and called the two Japanese American newspapers in town hoping that they might have this woman on their subscription lists. No luck. The Japanese American National Library[61] also didn't have any information. It seemed I had everyone involved in this search but no one had any leads.

Finally I decided to call "911." After conferring with her supervisor, the operator was able to tell me that the address I had was incorrect, but since I wasn't a relative or an immediate family member, she couldn't give me the correct address. I explained that even though I didn't know this woman, I had been asked to check on her and therefore felt responsible. All I wanted was to make sure she was all right. The operator said she would send the police to investigate.

I returned home, feeling helpless. I dialed the number I had three more times, and a woman finally answered. She was the woman we were searching for. The phone had rung many times before, she explained, but stopped before she could answer it. She admitted she was having chest pains. I asked for her address, which turned out to be five blocks from where we were looking. I offered to go over at once and suggested she go to the hospital. She refused and said she didn't want any help. I tried to convince her to call her doctor or, at the very least, let me call her doctor for her. She said she had none. She apparently had a few relatives but didn't want me to contact them either. I gave her my name and phone number and asked her to call me if she needed anything. I was at a complete loss.

A couple of weeks passed, and I tried contacting this woman again to see how she was doing. Again she said she was having pains and had to hang up. I was saddened to learn that she passed away a short time later. Although I didn't know anything about her at the time — whether she had a spouse or children, or any details of her redress case — I found out after her death that she had been a member of a rather prominent and well-known family.

Some cases I worked on took time to complete, particularly those involving veterans.

I worked with 442nd veteran Shig Doi on two redress cases involving veterans who lived in remote rural areas in the southwest. During one of their vacations, Shig and his wife decided to look up two of his war buddies who he thought might be living in the areas they were visiting. They inquired at a local veteran's administration hospital to see if either of his friends was on file there. Ironically, it turned out that one of them had an appointment that very day. Shig located the other veteran and told him of the redress program. Neither veteran knew a thing about the redress movement.

Upon returning from his vacation, Shig asked me to send applications to these two men right away. They returned their completed applications to me to look over. One veteran resided in a place called Dairy Creek, California, which was apparently an old gold mining area, the other in a small town in New Mexico. The Dairy Creek veteran received his redress check with no problem. He sent me a small amount of gold dust along with a thank you letter. Shig told me this veteran lives in an area so remote that it takes two hours to get to his post office box. Because of the distance, he picks up his mail only once every two weeks.

The case of the veteran in New Mexico was more problematic. His request for redress was repeatedly denied based on what later turned out to be misinformation. This veteran had joined the United States military long before many Japanese Americans. He worked on a military base as an airplane mechanic prior to the war. After Pearl Harbor was bombed, he was fired from his job. He later enlisted and became a sergeant and a highly decorated veteran.

Shig and I wanted to do all that we could to help this veteran because he was ninety percent disabled from his war injuries. At the time we were working on his case, he weighed less than one hundred pounds and suffered from a prostate affliction as well as emphysema. Given his condition, this man was basically immobile. We tried to work as quickly as we could, but the distance separating us slowed us down. We prepared his forms and assisted him in the appeals process. Shig and I discussed his case with ORA legal counsel Tink Cooper during one of her visits to San Francisco. Shig was extremely helpful in this case especially because this was his friend. He wanted very much to see this man get his long-deserved check.

In 1995, when ORA Administrator Bob Bratt visited San Francisco, I brought up this case, explaining that an incorrect address this man had used during the war contributed to the ORA denying him eligibility. Bob took down all the information. The ORA called me soon after and said, "Sox, are you sitting down?" I cautiously said, "Yes," thinking they were going to tell me they had denied this veteran's appeal. "Well, here's another one you can chalk up!" Shig and I were overjoyed!

After explaining to the ORA that this vet couldn't leave the trailer where he lived, they sent his check to his doorstep via

Federal Express. ORA went beyond the call of duty. Bob and his staff really put their heart into these cases.

On a bittersweet note, Jeff Adachi, a San Francisco public defender and fellow member of the San Francisco JACL, and I saw another difficult case through completion. It involved a veteran who had been denied redress. After three years of appeals and waiting for an answer, this veteran was finally given approval and received his check. In the process of waiting, however, this man was diagnosed with Alzheimer's disease and placed in a nursing home. According to his wife, the one word he said repeatedly to his social worker before his condition deteriorated was "redress."

While feeling relieved that some veterans at least learned about redress, I remained worried about other Japanese Americans out there who may have been totally unaware of the program, particularly if they didn't subscribe to Japanese American newspapers or have much contact with other Nikkei. In too many instances, I'd run into former internees, ask if they had applied for redress, and get blank looks in return. They had no idea what I was talking about. Some friends would see me on the street and say, "How come no one told us about redress?" It was constantly in the Japanese American papers, I told them, and added with a smile, "The cost of a subscription is worth twenty thousand dollars." There have been many times when I wished I could get on a truck with a bullhorn and announce the program to the world.

Each time I can put a check mark next to cases that I have completed, I can't describe the feeling. It's like a challenge that I was able to meet. You simply can't put a price on that kind of feeling.

Kudos to the ORA

My work was really made easier because of the wonderful working relationship I had over the years with the ORA office staff. My first contact person there was Alicie West Simpson (now living in Holland), who was in the operations section. I couldn't have asked for a more sensitive and conscientious person to work with me. She had a fantastic memory for details and specifics. We worked as a team and spoke to each other on a near daily basis, becoming long-distance friends in the process. Alicie kept records of all my cases on her desk, which sped things up. She usually reviewed my pending cases and gave me continual updates. Our standing joke was that we spent breakfast together every morning over a cup of coffee — with her in D.C. and me in San Francisco.

Joanne Chiedi, a litigation attorney, and I also talked nearly everyday about cases. We often discussed the pros and cons of complicated cases. It really helped to bounce ideas off of her and get needed legal advice.

I'm most grateful to have developed not only a close working relationship but also a personal friendship with Bob Bratt and Paul Suddes. Their offices were always accessible, and they assisted me in innumerable ways. After a time, I even phoned them at home or on their vacations. Bob worked extremely hard, with dedication and compassion, taking it upon himself to right the wrongs of the past and to implement an unprecedented program. Despite the monumental nature of the job, he was resourceful and innovative in applying his expertise. I don't know of any other government office or staff who would make an ordinary citizen feel so warmly welcomed.

Third Payment Period: October 1992

Just when Japanese Americans thought they had cleared all the hurdles, the government learned that it had underestimated the number of surviving internees. Instead of some sixty thousand eligible recipients, the number was actually closer to eighty thousand. Part of the reason was that Japanese have a longer life expectancy than Caucasians, so actuarial data used to calculate the number of potential recipients were inaccurate. In all likelihood further legislation was going to be required to pay the remaining number of eligibles, because the Civil Liberties Act of 1988 was capped in the amount of monies that could be allocated.

H.R. 4551 and S.2553 — the "Civil Liberties Act Amendments of 1992" —
were introduced in March 1992 for the purpose of extending benefits to cover the
remaining recipients. In September, 1992, both chambers passed the legislation by
voice vote, and on September 27, 1992, President Bush signed H.R. 4551 (P.L.
102-371) into law. In addition to increasing the amount of funds authorized by the
Civil Liberties Act of 1988 by four hundred million dollars, a new group of eligible
redress recipients was created: non-Japanese American spouses and parents who
were evacuated or interned. About half of the eighty people who fell into these cate-
gories were still alive. [62]

Thank goodness Congress saw fit to fulfill its promise of
redress by passing the Civil Liberties Act Amendments. Our community had had more than its share of obstacles and setbacks. We
could keep moving forward.

Assisting applicants during the third round of payments kept
me as busy as ever. In addition to helping the youngest eligible
recipients in this payment period, I also spent time helping individuals with special cases. These involved children born outside
of the camps or prohibited zones and, by law, were not eligible
for redress except under extenuating circumstances. In some of
these cases, pregnant mothers who left the camps on temporary
leave, perhaps to visit their husbands serving in the military, gave
birth and then returned to the camps. Under the law, their children would normally not be eligible for redress. Fortunately,
there were no blanket denials on cases like these. Each case was
individually reviewed and evaluated.

The number of tedious and time-consuming cases grew; several of these cases took more than a year of work. It was like trying to solve a jigsaw puzzle without having all the pieces.
Applicants could only sit tight and wait. I and others had been
doing a lot of research consulting resources such as the U.S.
Department of the Navy, the Bancroft Library at the University
of California at Berkeley, the War Relocation Authority records
section, and even the British Broadcasting Corporation in
England, which had some information on a special case I was

working on. The work fascinated me, but progress was very slow.

While in the midst of research, I got to see Aiko Herzig-Yoshinaga during a stopover in San Francisco. A noted historian and researcher, Aiko consulted for the ORA. I wanted her thoughts and opinions about the chances of gaining approval for some of our cases. She was realistic. It's going to be a long haul, she said. I told her that I intended to go as far as I possibly could with these cases and hoped that the Department of Justice would simply give the benefit of the doubt to these individuals. Aiko patted me on the shoulder and said, "Good for you, Sox." I felt I just couldn't give up. Not then, and not now.

Issues we hadn't anticipated surfaced. Trying to find answers to complex questions took a good deal of time. For example, about one hundred Japanese Americans in Hawai`i had applied for redress but their claims were refused. Research had recently been uncovered which showed that during the war only Japanese Americans were removed from, and not allowed to return to, an area in Hawai`i called Wai`au. This group sought to prove that they had been deprived of their liberty.

Additionally, cases involving children of voluntary evacuees, seasonal laborers, railroad workers, Peruvian and other Latin Americans of Japanese descent forcibly deported to the U.S. and interned as hostages,[63] and children who relocated to Japan with their parents during the war, began coming to the fore. In the first and last categories, it was argued that minor children had no choice or say in the matter and should therefore not be punished for the actions of their parents. Seasonal laborers and railroad workers faced difficulty proving their places of residence during the war since their jobs were transient by nature. All things considered, we had more than enough to keep us busy in 1994.

Fiftieth Anniversary of the 442nd Regimental Combat Team

I went on vacation in the spring to attend the 442nd Regimental Combat Team's fiftieth anniversary reunion in Honolulu, Hawai`i, which was held March 24-28, 1993. I was a guest of the Cannon Company of the 442nd. The size of the crowds attending the events was outstanding: some twenty-seven hundred people attended the first banquet alone. It was an emotionally draining week.

Watching the 442nd veterans parade through the heart of Waikiki, in full view of tourists and islanders alike, I experienced a surge of pride. They deserved every accolade. The memorial service at the National Memorial Cemetery of the Pacific (Punchbowl) was extremely moving and beautiful. All of the programs went well. It was a rousing tribute to our Japanese American veterans, many of whom felt this was their last big hurrah.

The week passed quickly. Upon returning to San Francisco, the redress office contacted me to help mail hundreds of postcards to individuals born during the years 1943 to 1945. Although these individuals had applied for redress, they hadn't complied with the ORA's request for additional information. I sent off the postcards and then tried to phone each person, urging them to contact the ORA in order to receive their payments. It is a complete mystery to me why some people procrastinated.

Of the seventy-five thousand people who had been paid, the checks of only two were either stolen or lost. One of those missing checks was eventually accounted for. An impressive record indeed!

Our work on redress was far from over. Many cases in the third round remained unresolved and on appeal. In May 1993, a community meeting with ORA representatives Paul (Suddes) and Tink (Cooper) was held in Japantown. About sixty people turned out. Paul explained the various categories of eligibility and discussed ORA's policies. It was a tiring and stressful day for him. People's frustrations showed as they asked him to change the regulations even though neither he nor the ORA can make laws. They only administer them.

The NCRR steeled itself for the likelihood that it might take another legislative bill or more congressional support to address these issues. We decided to send letters to then-new Attorney General Janet Reno and request a meeting to discuss the Department of Justice policies.

Coalition Lobbying trip: August 1993

On August 2, 1993, I traveled with members of the NCRR and JACL to Washington, D.C. to further discuss with James Turner, U.S. Assistant Attorney General, and Paul (Suddes) the special cases of eligibility. We didn't get a meeting with Attorney General Reno after all. There were four of us from the Bay Area: Grace Shimizu, of the Peruvian Japanese History Project;[64] John Ota and me from NCRR; and Pat Okamoto, a concerned citizen whose husband was born outside of the camps and denied redress. We hoped to reverse some of the denial cases, or, in the very least, get a re-review.

Our meeting with Mr. Turner went well. He was a sympathetic listener and a patient man. Although we were scheduled to meet with him for an hour and a half, he said from the outset that if we needed more time that was fine with him. We felt at ease with him. We discussed the issue of minor children who had been taken to Japan by their parents during the war; women who had left the camps temporarily, given birth, and then reentered (about eighty cases); Peruvian Japanese; and others.

After the meeting I spoke informally with Mr. Turner, who recalled our NCRR lobbying trip four years ago when we presented him with a string of folded paper cranes. He was referring to the trip we made in August 1989, to lobby for an increase in appropriations. We had met then with various members of Congress and Mr. Turner. He smiled and remarked that he still had the cranes in his office.

The following day we visited with Representative Mineta, who, despite being inundated with meetings, gave us all the time we needed. The timing wasn't ideal. Capitol Hill was engrossed in discussions over the federal budget, while the Justice Department was focused on the Rodney King case. Despite all the activity, we met with the aides of California Representative Matsui, Rep. Don Edwards, and Sen. Dianne Feinstein, and talked in person with Senator Inouye.

We left Washington feeling optimistic that the Justice Department would rule favorably on these issues. Nothing was definite, either way. Cases would be reviewed one by one. That's all we could ask for.

After returning to San Francisco, I continued to plug away, speaking frequently with Tink in the ORA about my denial cases and hoping to present compelling enough information. Perhaps more than any other lobbying trip, I felt positive about this last one. I hoped we would receive good news and give closure to these cases.

The Japanese American press covered our trip to D.C., and, as a result, I received daily phone calls from individuals across the country who had read about our efforts and worried about their chances for success. Several individuals who fell into these special categories told me they hadn't even considered applying for redress, thinking they had had no chance. I couldn't stress to them enough that there was no disgrace in being turned down and that they should at least try. The trip also generated considerable interest from the mainstream media wanting to learn more about the internment of Peruvian Japanese and other Latin American Japanese. Reporters called, saying they could find no information on this "new" group of internees. We explained that these cases were more complex because they involved immigration agencies and records. Grace (Shimizu) and Art Shibayama, a former Japanese Peruvian internee, appeared on CNN to discuss this neglected history. Redress and reparations for Peruvian Japanese have been discussed for years, but stories about their experiences have only recently surfaced.

As of this writing, a federal bill has been introduced (The Wartime Parity and Justice Act of 2001) by Sen. Daniel Inouye (S. 1237) and U.S. House of Rep. Xavier Becerra to provide 1) forty-five million dollars in public education funding to fulfill the education mandate of the Civil Liberties Act of 1988; 2) redress for Japanese Americans who were denied reparations under the Civil Liberties Act of 1988 for technical reasons; and, 3) redress for Japanese Latin Americans who suffered civil and human rights violations by the U.S. government during World War II.

XII

TOPAZ REVISITED: 1993

I revisited my past during Labor Day weekend 1993, when I traveled to Topaz, Utah. I hadn't been back there since the day Tom and I left in 1945. I was excited about this pilgrimage, and my sister-in-law Margaret Ouye accompanied me. We learned that over two hundred and fifty people had signed up for the trip. On the agenda was a visit to the camp site, as well as the town of Delta.

Over the years, I had seen some of the people from those Topaz years, former internees as well as former administrators. In September 1992, I had attended a Topaz reunion, which was held in Burlingame, California. I was still working on the NCRR letter-writing campaign at the time, so I was there soliciting letters. I saw people I hadn't seen in years. Arts and crafts made in Topaz filled an entire room. Roscoe Bell, who had been the camp's assistant director, attended the reunion. He and his wife had stayed in touch with a number of former internees. In fact, my friend Harry Konda paid a visit to the Bells at their Pacific Northwest home. Harry was genuinely moved to see a picture of my sister-in-law Yo and her husband Roy sitting on their mantel. Yo had been Mr. Bell's secretary in the camps.

I looked forward to seeing my former boss Claude Pratt and his wife on this pilgrimage. We had kept in contact with one another since 1945, even though I hadn't seen them in years. They remembered me every Christmas with a card and a family update. They now resided in Ogden, Utah, and had corresponded with me to let me know they were planning to attend. Due to an illness at the last minute, however, they were unable to go. I was disappointed by the news but hoped that they were all right. Claude and his wife had felt compassion for Japanese Americans. Each time I spoke with him, Claude made it a point to apologize for what had happened to us during the war. He was glad that we finally received a governmental apology and reparations.

Several signs and arrows directed the way to the camp. I felt slightly anxious as we rode along. No physical remnants of our former camp remained, yet there were things about Topaz that were all too familiar. After nearly fifty years, it still felt like we were far removed from civilization. The place was overgrown with sagebrush and weeds. The scorching heat and dust enveloped us. We were handed a map of the original site. I couldn't visualize where everything stood fifty years ago even though I had spent over three years of my life there.

People fanned out across the site. I happened to meet the camp-born daughter of a woman from my old hometown. She was anxious to see Topaz again, to look upon the place where she was born and raised. She studied the map and figured out the location of the camp hospital. She stood in its place, bending over to touch the ground. I watched her pick up a few pebbles for souvenirs and then walk over to the area where her block had been, alone in her memories.

I wanted to see the historical monument erected in remembrance of the camp. We learned it had been vandalized more than once with gunshots. As we stood before it, I felt a sense of pride. Here was something lasting which would teach people about the camp and its history. America's history. It stood as a testament to the past.

We toured the town of Delta and were amazed to find that after the war townspeople had purchased the barracks we lived in. Many of the barracks had been converted into homes after first being sectioned off since they were too long to haul as is. One family had bought one of the barracks for fifteen hundred dollars and had lived in it for thirty-five years. It was interesting to see what the residents had done with our former living quarters. Some had added on rooms and porches, lowered windows, added kitchens, and fixed them up quite nicely. Others were landscaped with gardens and picket fences. That was an odd sight to see.

I wished that my grandson Aaron had been old enough to take along on this pilgrimage. I hope one day he will have an opportunity to visit Topaz and learn the history behind it. Plans are underway to build a museum there, which will incorporate one of the original barracks. That fills me with hope that younger generations of Americans will have a concrete reminder to not repeat the mistakes of the past.

The first week of November 1993 was an uplifting one. Paul (Suddes) of the ORA and I frequently contacted each other regarding several of my pending cases. He called me from his home, after returning from a trip, to give me some good news: some of my tougher cases had been resolved in a positive way.

One of those cases involved an unemployed man. His application was approved, and he received his redress check in December: a timely Christmas present for him and his family.

I was encouraged to learn from the ORA that as of December 27, 1993, seventy-nine thousand, one hundred and fifty-five people had received their redress checks. There was enough money to pay an additional nine hundred people through the month of January.

Going to Jail

On July of 1994, I embarked on yet another search for a former internee. My track record was pretty good. Maybe that's why these cases came my way.

The ORA had made several attempts to contact a gentleman who had applied for redress back in 1991. This man was apparently homeless and could therefore not furnish an acceptable address. I was asked to help track him down. From the information they received, the ORA believed this man still lived in Northern California.

I placed ads in the local Japanese American newspapers and called area churches to see if anyone knew of this man or his whereabouts. Almost instantly, I received a call from the San Jose JACL office. This man had had a run-in with the law and had been paroled from jail after serving a light sentence. They didn't know his current whereabouts, though.

I then heard from Richard Konda of the Asian Law Alliance [65] in San Jose that this same man just five months prior, in February, had contacted him via a third party. This man wanted help in submitting another redress application because he hadn't heard back from the ORA. It was this second application, which had a Union City, California postmark, that had prompted the ORA to contact me. The Law Alliance directed me to the Vacaville correctional facility, where I learned that this individual, arrested again, was serving time.

This information startled me, and I decided I needed some legal advice before I ventured any further. I turned to my friend Jeff Adachi. I wanted to know what was entailed in getting this man his twenty thousand dollars if he was in jail. Would I need to get his permission to pursue his case on his behalf ? Since I wasn't serving in any official capacity, this complicated matters, Jeff advised. He suggested we meet with this man in person.

As a lawyer, Jeff could arrange an appointment at the Vacaville facility and he did just that. He gave the officials our names, and we arranged to go to the facility at the end of August. The night before our meeting, I had trouble falling asleep. I had no idea what to expect, having never stepped foot in a prison before. Mostly, I wondered how this man would receive us.

Finding the prison took longer than we anticipated. We got lost and spent an hour looking for it. At last we found it. I guess I expected to see a scary place, but it was surprisingly ordinary. We went through a tight security check at the entrance. Guards told us the man we were meeting worked on the prison grounds and had to finish his job first. We waited for over an hour before he was finally brought in to see us.

We walked single file into a room, led by a female guard, who locked the door behind us. She then left the room and instructed us to rap on the window when we were done. I felt a little nervous about being locked in, but I was relieved to see before me a man who looked healthy and fit. He looked like he was in his fifties. I'm embarrassed to say that I had envisioned someone far different, someone who looked menacing. As we spoke, I realized he was a highly intelligent and articulate person who felt badly about what he had done. He repeatedly apologized, saying his life was ruined. He had lost touch with his family about twenty-five years ago. He was ashamed and embarrassed about what he had done, and it was clear that he still thought about his family. Jeff and I tried our best to console and convince him that because he was still young, he could start his life over upon his release. I suggested that once he was free, he should consider contacting his family again, to let them know he was alive. He said he was too embarrassed and that his mother would be upset if she heard that he had been in jail. I said that if he at least called to let them know he was okay, his mom might not react the way he thought. And if his family says they would disown him, he should accept it and cross them off the list. You won't have to worry about them anymore, I said.

We spent about forty-five minutes talking with him and going over the necessary ORA forms. We completed everything.

Before we left, I couldn't help but encourage this man to keep out of trouble and not make things harder on himself. Build yourself back up, your self-esteem and your character, I told him. In time, you'll feel better about yourself. The fact that he felt embarrassed about what he had done is a good thing. It says something about him. He was scheduled to be paroled in less than a month. I told him that given the information I had, he could probably expect to receive his redress check in October and that maybe this would help him get back on his feet. He wrote down the telephone number of a friend he would be staying with once he was paroled and handed it to me. We wished him well and headed back to San Francisco.

Jeff was the epitome of patience that day and of immense help. It had taken better than half the day to complete this "mission." I'm very glad he was there with me.

On October 14, the ORA called to tell me that this man had received his redress check. Were it not for the help of the San Jose JACL, the Asian Law Alliance, and Jeff Adachi, this case couldn't have been completed. I called the number this man had given me and spoke with his friend, who relayed the message that this man had been so happy to receive the redress money. One day soon after I received a call from this individual at Kimochi, where I volunteer. He thanked me and Jeff for helping him out. It was good to hear from him, and I reminded him to keep his nose clean. I probably sounded stern, but I felt like a mother to him in some way. Hopefully, the money helped change his life for the better.

In 1994, Jeff, I and the JACL-San Francisco chapter began helping the children of Japanese American U.S. Navy language school instructors attain redress. These children were denied redress on the basis that they hadn't been subjected to the internment camps. As a chapter, we decided to request help from the national JACL. Jeff drafted a formal letter to Randy Senzaki, then national director. In response, Randy asked Jeff to handle the case. Jeff immediately got to work, developing a thirty-page brief that we sent to the new U.S. Assistant Attorney General for Civil Rights, Deval Patrick, and to Paul Suddes.

Our strategy was to request a meeting with Mr. Patrick, which Karen Narasaki, then JACL Washington, D.C. representative, helped arrange.

Coalition Lobbying Trip: September, 1994

On September 19, 1994, John Ota, Grace Shimizu, Jeff Adachi, Miya Iwataki, Kay Ochi, and I traveled to Washington, D.C. to meet with Mr. Patrick. We represented groups such as NCRR, JACL, and the Japanese Peruvian Oral History Project. We also met with DeDe Green, the new ORA administrator. DeDe had worked with Bob Bratt for over a decade in several agencies and knew a lot about redress. She was definitely on top of things, which made us feel good right from the start.

We wanted to discuss cases which we had earlier raised with the ORA and Department of Justice: children born in intern-ment camps to "visiting" mothers (*e.g.,* children of 442nd RCT members); minor children sent back to Japan with their parents; Hawai`i cases; Japanese Peruvians forcibly uprooted from Peru and brought to the United States for possible hostage exchanges; and children born in Boulder, Colorado, to military language school instructors (about seventeen of them). We hoped to get reversals on some of the ORA's earlier decisions.

Each of us spoke on a different category; Jeff summarized everything. I gave the human side of the story regarding Navy language school children. I related to Mr. Patrick the hardships inflicted on those Japanese Americans who had moved to Colorado to assist the U.S. Navy in teaching Japanese to its offi-cers. They really had no choice but to help, because how could any American refuse the government? At the same time, given the uncertainty of the war and our own government's distrust of us, it hadn't been an easy decision to make. These Japanese Americans chose patriotism first, I stressed, and subjected their families to harassment and racism in Boulder. They were paid so little for what they did there that a number of them depleted their life's savings in order to survive. I cried as I spoke and was embarrassed when Mr. Patrick quietly asked one of his staffers to go and get me some tissue, but I was speaking from my heart. I wanted to emphasize that these families made sacrifices that had to be taken into consideration.

We spoke for nearly two hours, more time than we had planned. Mr. Patrick was warm and clearly committed to working with us on this issue. Past meetings between him and representatives of our community had already resulted in some reversals of ORA denials. We departed feeling upbeat and encouraged that he would interpret the regulations more broadly.

With the end of the redress program on the horizon — the ORA office was to close on August 10, 1998 — we in NCRR discussed our future direction. We debated whether to change our name to reflect a more progressive and broader organization. We spent a lot of time at one meeting trying to figure out another name which would fit the letters N-C-R-R. I laugh in thinking about that meeting because we came up with some pretty crazy names. I opposed changing our name, especially with the redress program still in place. I felt it's not right to change midstream because then all our hard work to build up the NCRR and its reputation will have been for naught.

XIII

EDUCATING THE YOUNG

I've always felt strongly that educating people, particularly children, about the internment can go a long way in ensuring that it never happens again to any group of people. I continue to speak at schools and with students whenever I can.

One school visit was especially memorable because the school is located near the area where I grew up. Mr. Paul DeWitt, a social studies teacher at Newark Memorial High School, invited me to speak to his class. He annually presents innovative programs on intolerance and devotes a good deal of time to the Japanese American internment. Mr. DeWitt has made a difference, and he has invited me back several times to Memorial High.

I think most of us former internees would agree that education about the internment is extremely important and an ongoing goal. Bay Area schools have a strong interest in the internment. Some schools I've visited even incorporate cultural activities in their internment lessons.

For example, nearly fifty students from a private school in Palo Alto visited Japantown one day. The class was made up predominantly of upper class, white students. The students learned about the camp experience, viewed pictures, and heard firsthand accounts. They came to the local Japanese American community center, where I led a demonstration in sushi-making. The center staff and volunteers presented other cultural demonstrations to round out the afternoon. Some of the students came up to me and said that it was the best field trip they had ever had. I hope their interest in both Japanese and Japanese American history grows.

I've had the privilege of speaking at The Hamlin School, a private girl's school in San Francisco. For the first time in my life, someone asked for my autograph. I was stunned. The class had been studying about Topaz, Utah, and I came to describe camp life. Meeting an actual former internee from Topaz made the story real to the children. I'm encouraged that schools, both public and private, are taking an interest.

I have also spoken, and continue to speak, on college campuses about the internment. I really enjoy doing this. Whenever I'm asked, I try to help students with their theses or papers. It is an honor having young people take an interest in my life and what I have to say. It saddens me when they tell me they didn't learn anything about America's concentration camps until college.

It is critical to educate our young about the past so that they can help mold a better future. Children are highly perceptive and understand much more than we adults credit them. Youngsters have often asked me if I think they or their parents could someday be put in camps because of their ancestry. I tell them we must remember what our Constitution stands for and to make sure that our rights are always protected and safeguarded, so that no group will ever experience what we did. I remind them that we have to be most vigilant in times of war and chaos.

Before concluding one of my talks at a school, I asked the teacher if I could pass on a few words of advice to the students. At this point in my life, I said, I regret not knowing more about my own parents' life. What was their childhood like? What did they enjoy doing? What kind of things were important to them? I wasn't curious enough to ask those kinds of questions when I was younger. I encouraged these students to sit down with their parents and talk with them, to ask questions and be willing to listen. If you don't do this with your parents or older family members, I said, you'll lose a sense of your own history. Maybe forever. And it is so important to know your roots.

The NCRR's goal of including the internment experience in school textbooks and curriculum continued. Toward that end, we were involved in advocacy issues with the California Department of Education and conducted workshops to help teachers understand the lessons of the internment. One of our workshops, held in March 1992, attracted over one hundred educators. Lucy Hamai chaired this event, which included speakers such as Fred Korematsu, who resisted the internment and who, in 1998, received the country's highest civilian award, the Presidential Medal of Freedom; Kiyoshi Yoshii, a member of the 442nd Regimental Combat Team; Victor Ohashi, a schoolteacher in San Francisco; and myself. The teachers seemed genuinely enthusiastic about the subject. We hope they have implemented lesson plans and materials which address this history.

There have been other efforts in our city to teach the general public about the internment. In addition to presentations in February, many of my speaking engagements center on the month of May, federally designated as "Asian Pacific American Heritage Month." I've noticed more public and private organizations and companies are interested in hearing about our history. I've received requests to speak about the internment and the redress movement from diverse places, such as the U.S. Mint in San Francisco, the San Francisco Police Academy, and even a culinary arts school in the city.

I had the opportunity to participate in a ceremony to commemorate the former site of the Tanforan Detention Camp. In its place today stands the Tanforan Park Shopping Center, where the NCRR-San Francisco held its first Day of Remembrance program.

The shopping center's owner had earlier moved into storage a large bronze replica of Seabiscuit, a prize-winning racehorse that had run at the Tanforan racetrack prior to World War II.

Along with the replica was a plaque denoting the site as a former wartime detention center for Japanese Americans. Due to renovations at the center, the statue and plaque had been temporarily removed from public display.

The NCRR received numerous calls from friends and strangers, who wondered why Seabiscuit and the historic plaque were removed. Ironically, at about the same time I was contemplating starting a petition to have the horse and plaque restored to public view, Mike Hegadus, a local TV news reporter, contacted me for an interview. We drove to the Tanforan Park Shopping Center, where he videotaped me along with some camp mementos, which I had borrowed from a friend.

During the filming I met the manager of the center. He invited us into his office. On the wall he had pictures of Seabiscuit as well as an overview of the former racetrack. I used the opportunity to inquire about the statue and happily learned that the shopping center had plans to bring Seabiscuit and the plaque out of storage. In fact, he said, a rededication ceremony for the permanent display of the horse and several other plaques would take place in the center's parking lot.

A special ceremony was held at the shopping center in 1991. The statue of Seabiscuit rests on a cement block encircled by three plaques, including one which describes the Tanforan Detention Center. An American flag flies overhead. Spotlights illuminate the horse so visitors can see it at night. The manager invited me to speak at this event as a former Tanforan internee. I thanked the center for promoting public awareness about what happened to Americans of Japanese ancestry in 1942. Many Japanese Americans and community supporters[66] turned out for this event, which was heartwarming.

Every year in February, NCRR holds an annual Day of Remembrance program at various locations in the city. We held one remembrance at the Center for the Arts at Yerba Buena Gardens in conjunction with AsianImprov aRts, a jazz group.

Over four hundred people attended that program, one of our largest gatherings ever. I worried each year that since most people have received their redress checks, interest will drop. I'm glad I'm proven wrong. Younger generations of Japanese Americans are showing an interest in participating and remembering. The event continues to succeed.

As public knowledge and interest about Japanese Americans grow, I feel I shouldn't ignore any opportunity to speak out on issues. Although it recalls such unhappy times when I talk about the war and that part of my life, I feel it is vitally important to educate the public. In turn, talking about the camp experience helps heal some of the pain.

XIV

END OF THE ROAD TO REDRESS

Sox was invited to deliver a speech at the closing ceremony of the Office of Redress Administration on September 10, 1998, in the Great Hall of Justice, Washington, D.C. Ten years after the Civil Liberties Act of 1988 was signed, more than eighty-one thousand eligible internees received their redress checks. The text of Sox's speech follows:

Good morning, Attorney General Janet Reno, members of Congress, distinguished guests and friends. Sen. "Sparky" Matsunaga is here with us in spirit.

I was asked to speak briefly about my experience.

On May 9, 1942, I became citizen 21373. My mother, three adult brothers and I were evacuated to Tanforan Racetrack where we were greeted by armed guards and surrounded with barbed wire fences. We were physically searched like criminals. In the process, our neatly packed suitcases were tipped over in search of contrabands.

Our first meal consisted of discolored cold cuts, overcooked swiss chard and moldy bread. I refused it. A horsestall, twenty by nine feet, with manure on the floor was assigned to us. We were ordered to fill sacks with straw for our mattress.

That night, I cried myself to sleep and said to myself, "I can't believe I'm in America."

A three-sided makeshift toilet with no door was situated on the pathway to the messhall. A gentleman donated his precious underwear that covered us from the waist up. Some camps had raw sewage running in front of the stables.

After four months, an old, dusty, gas-lamped train took us to Topaz, Utah, a desolate sagebrush-laden camp. Shades were drawn throughout our trip until we reached Salt Lake. Topaz, Utah was to be our home for an indefinite time. We were shocked to see there were no doors in the latrines. No privacy, no partitions in our barracks, no furniture. A potbelly stove and one naked light bulb served the entire family.

We were fed innards of animals until we complained. We again suffered psychological stress of confinement.

For many young people, life stopped in mid-career. They were immobilized for lack of purpose. Traditionally strong family ties were broken. Parents lost control of their children. Fathers lost their status and were no longer the breadwinners.

We endured over one hundred degrees in the summers and ten-twenty degrees below in the winters.

The camps went smoothly, until the loyalty questionnaire and questions #27 and #28 were issued, a proof of loyalty to serve on combat duty wherever ordered. Internees were outraged. Those who resisted wanted their Constitutional rights restored and their families released from camp. Mothers cried and begged their sons not to go. "We lost everything to evacuation - we are too old to begin life anew without you," they cried. It was a trying period for all concerned. They said, "But if you must go, don't try to be a hero, and do not bring shame to the family." Japanese Americans served with distinction.

NCRR's first lobbying trip was in 1984. We were nervous, we knew nothing about lobbying. But Congressman Barney Frank gave us a much needed shot in the arm when he said, "Don't waste your time on me... I'm for it... go after the others." Our efforts intensified. Over twenty-five thousand letters and over four hundred mailgrams were sent to Congress and the President. We had many ups and downs, but we persevered.

Finally, on August 10, 1988, the Civil Liberties Act of 1988, enacted by Congress and signed into law by President Ronald

Reagan, acknowledged the fundamental injustice of the World War II incarceration of Japanese Americans. But the appropriation was inadequate — we leaned heavily on our Japanese American congressional representatives for encouragement. They gave us strength to continue our fight. We were losing so many former internees so fast.

Our efforts were not in vain. Finally, on October 9, 1990, I witnessed the first check presentation by Attorney General Richard Thornburgh, who said to each of the nine recipients, "I'm sorry it took so long."

Congress apologized on behalf of the nation. America had shown its greatness.

We thank the Commission on Wartime Relocation and Internment of Civilians for providing us the opportunity to prove our right to redress. Our thanks to the Office of Redress Administration — Bob Bratt, the first administrator, who left his footprints in our hearts; to Paul Suddes, Alicie Simpson, DeDe Greene, Joanne Chiedi, Lisa Johnson, Tink Cooper, and Emi Kuboyama for their cordial assistance with redress cases — the homeless, cases in Japan, the physically-impaired that required special attention, providing color coded-forms to avoid confusion — and in many, many situations went beyond the call of duty.

We owe a debt of gratitude for the endless support from the community, from people of all races, and all walks of life. You made redress a reality. The closure of the camps created resettlement problems far greater than the evacuation. I had no home to go back to and had only what I brought with me from the camp. Storage places were ransacked; ugly signs greeted us. Our parents, who suffered the most, took it on the chin, shared tiny rooms with others, lived in storefronts, or church auditoriums. Frightening Night Riders[67] targeted those who returned to their homes.

Perhaps it was these stories that roused the conscience of third-generation Japanese Americans to seek restitution for their parents and grandparents who were traumatized.

We cannot undo history, but let us continue to make the lessons of the past serve as a beacon to protect civil rights for all and that the Civil Liberties Public Education Fund grant program will continue to illuminate the true and accurate history surrounding the exclusion, forced removal and internment of Japanese Americans during World War II.

I am truly humbled. Thank you for this privilege and for allowing me to share in your glory.

I love you all!

XV

Giving Back

In many ways my life really began after I retired in 1981. With Alan graduating from college and Tom's passing, I had time on my hands. I needed to find something to fill the void. And since I cannot bear the thought of sitting at home and watching soap operas, getting involved in the Japanese American community proved a welcomed relief. In addition to my work on redress, I'm grateful to have had the opportunity to do volunteer work with various community organizations. It has truly enriched my life.

I credit my friend Sandy Ouye Mori for motivating me and teaching me what volunteer work is all about. I learned a lot from her because she has a certain way with volunteers. Sandy has a knack for getting people involved and having them feel good about it.

Kimochi, Inc. (loosely translated, meaning "feeling" in Japanese) has played such a prominent role in my life, and the lives of others. I began my volunteer work with this organization. Later I also did much of my one-on-one community work on redress cases there.

Kimochi is a community-based organization which provides services for Japanese American elderly. Back in 1971 — largely through the efforts of the third generation, the Sansei — Kimochi was born. It humbly began when a few Sansei volunteers in the community offered to help Issei fill out their Social Security forms. From there, other services were added: a safety escort service to and from Japantown; a library of materials and resources in Japanese;

a social lounge; and a general information and referral project housed in the Japan Trade Center, which sits in the heart of redeveloped Japantown. People like Steve Nakajo, Kimochi's executive director, nurtured the idea of the younger generation giving something back to their elders.

Kimochi has grown into a multi-service organization, providing Japanese American seniors with residential care, social services, a daily nutrition and hot meals program, transportation, and social and recreational day care in San Francisco Japantown. Kimochi is not only a community focal point but is also a well known and highly respected organization in San Francisco and the greater Bay Area.

I first got involved in Kimochi through its fundraising efforts when, in 1980, the organization launched an ambitious project to raise one million three hundred thousand dollars. The goal was to build a residential, respite and adult day care home for older adults. Even though it was considered an enormous undertaking for the Nikkei community, I believed strongly in this project.

Sandy was the project coordinator then. After my retirement, I offered to volunteer in the Kimochi administrative office, where I typed proposals and correspondence. I respected Sandy's philosophy about the organization and recognized that she had vast knowledge and information at her fingertips. I wanted to be that kind of person: someone in the community to whom people could turn to for help.

In time, Kimochi raised enough money. When the framework of the Kimochi Home was finally erected, we held a community-wide celebration. I volunteered to make *mochi* to hand out to those in attendance. Together with my niece Connie Morita and her two daughters, we made over four hundred pieces of *mochi*. The Kimochi Home opened in February 1983.

I began to feel as though I was growing as an individual. Volunteering did that for me. I started spending my mornings at the nutrition program, which began in 1974, and my afternoons helping out in the administrative office. I was like a student, learning simply by being involved and surrounded by talented professionals. My father was right about community involvement: I learned something positive from those who were doing good things. The Sansei involved in making Kimochi a reality had tremendous drive and heart.

Today I remain involved with Kimochi in a variety of ways. In addition to serving on the board of directors, I volunteer five days a week at the nutrition program. The program is extremely successful and popular; on average we prepare food for as many as four hundred and thirty five people a day. In addition, we prepare eighty-five to one hundred home-delivered lunches daily. Kimochi's lunch program is unique because we serve hot Japanese meals every day of the year, including weekends and holidays. The program is open to any senior, not just Japanese Americans, over sixty years of age.

My son volunteers in the community too, and was in fact involved with Kimochi long before me. His son Aaron, my only grandchild, was born in 1983. I want to expose Aaron to the Nikkei community and to the idea of volunteer work. To that end, from the time Aaron was very young, I took him with me to the Kimochi nutrition program. I'm proud of the person he has become and hope that he will continue to give of himself to the community.

My other work with Kimochi involved nursing home visitations. Several of us — Louise Osada, Miyo Sera, Kimiko Toyota, Katherine Nunotani and I — visited Japanese patients at the San Francisco Community Convalescent Hospital for a number of years. For a while, we visited three other nursing homes in one day's time, but we found it impossible to make the rounds. A number of wheelchair-bound residents at San Francisco Convalescent formerly lived at Kimochi Home.

Knowing that the Japanese American residents there don't get to eat much Japanese food, the other women and I cooked foods for them. I empathized greatly with the few remaining Issei residents, who couldn't speak English. The language barrier made it difficult for them to communicate with others. We tried to ensure that their needs were taken care of, whether it meant acting as go-betweens on their behalf or running errands for them. I felt these patients enjoyed our visits, and I couldn't help but think that someday we may be in their shoes.

In this day and age, as with most other community-based organizations, fundraising for Kimochi is an ongoing activity and necessity. Kimochi has several fundraisers during the year, but its major vehicle, called "Sansei Live!," is a gala evening affair filled with music, dance and Japanese and American food.

The first "Sansei Live!" was held in October 1983. Nearly every year since then, I volunteer for this event, helping coordinate *sushi*-making by organizing a volunteer crew of about eighty people. It is a labor-intensive and time-consuming project because we prepare thousands of pieces of *sushi* for about fifteen hundred people. We all feel good about volunteering our time because it is for a worthy cause and the need simply exists.

In addition to Kimochi, I devoted my energies to the formation of a new group, the Asian American Arts Foundation.[68] This group was the brainchild of Jeff Adachi, my friend and fellow San Francisco–JACL board member.

The Foundation launched the "Golden Ring Award" in 1995. These awards recognized Asian Pacific American artists for their work in preserving our cultural heritage and provided grants to emerging artists. We wanted to highlight the fact that Asian Pacific Americans have considerable talent and have made significant contributions to society through the arts. It was a challenging event to undertake given the months of planning, fundraising, and outreach that were required, but I learned a great deal watching it develop and being part of its mission. I became the biggest "beggar" in the community by calling upon many individuals and businesses for donations.

I continue to remain involved in other community organizations such as the National Coalition for Redress and Reparations, Nihonmachi Legal Outreach, Japanese American Citizens League-San Francisco chapter, National Japanese American Historical Society, Asian Law Caucus,[69] and the Japanese Cultural and Community Center of Northern California.

I hope to pass on what I've learned to the younger generation so that they can carry on the spirit of volunteering. I value the opportunities I've had to work with many different organizations over the years. I'm so very proud of my community, and as long as I'm needed and can contribute something, I'll be there.

XVI

REFLECTIONS

I regret my entire family didn't live to see redress happen. In my heart I hope my parents would've been proud that I learned from them the importance of community involvement, and that, in my own way, I did my best to fight for justice and equality. I never sought accolades from my brothers and sisters, but I think they're proud of my part in this struggle.

My brother Hiss always encouraged me and expressed enthusiasm about my activism. He suggested on several occasions that our family travel to Japan after we got our redress money (my older brother Masao and I were the only ones who had never been to Japan). He didn't live to see his redress check. Winning redress was truly bittersweet because thousands and thousands of people, like Masao and Hiss, died before ever hearing the government apologize or receiving their reparations.

My family remains close knit. We spend holidays together and honor the traditions passed on to us by our parents and ancestors. We still celebrate every New Year's, Japanese American–style. On holidays I really understand the importance, but also feel the loss, of family members. Much like the New Year's of my childhood, my brother-in-law and his wife, Roy and Yo Kitashima, host an open house and invite a few dozen friends and relatives to share the day with them. We cook days ahead of time, preparing traditional, old-fashioned Japanese foods. Roy and Yo always have a generous spread. On the eve, we get together and eat *soba* (buckwheat noodles; symbolic of long life) and, with an American twist, toast with champagne. I hope the younger generations of our family will continue these traditions.

I also have something else to pass on to my grandson Aaron: a family crest, or *mon*. It saddens me that I never saw our *mon*, either my father's or my mother's. My interest in researching our family *mon* was stirred when my niece's daughter got married and wanted to know what our *mon* looked like. I had no idea. Two friends, Masi Nihei and Shiz Mihara, assisted me in my quest. I read about the history of *mon*. I looked up my mother's maiden name, Ishimaru, because that would be the *mon* I would pass on. I found it. It resembles three round rocks. Shiz suggested that I create my own crest to pass on to Aaron. I designed a fan because it symbolizes something which is expanding all the time, like how I want to be as a person. Within the fan I incorporated my mother's *mon* and so now I finally have a family crest. This will be Aaron's link to the past.

In looking back at the years since my retirement, NCRR's the greatest thing that ever happened for me. I think, or hope, that we lobbied for redress in a respectable, straightforward manner. We didn't lose our belief in the absolute power of perseverance. If you think you're doing the right thing, the main thing is to persevere. If you don't keep on trying, what you believe in dies right there.

All of us who labored in this struggle learned by doing because the redress movement had no precedence. We learned about the political process and what it took to spur our Congress and the President into action. Nothing was handed to us on a plate. Nothing of value ever comes easily. I'll never forget that.

We as Japanese Americans accomplished three things. First, as a minority group, we persuaded our government to apologize and admit its mistakes. Second, getting redress designated as an entitlement program on par with Medicare and Social Security was monumental. Many in our own community don't realize how long and how hard an effort it was to enact a redress bill. And last of all, it took the efforts of every person to achieve redress. We're grateful to our Japanese American members of Congress and the accomplishments of the Japanese American veterans. People of all different races and from all walks of life, however, helped us win the struggle. It takes unity to make change.

My fervent hope is that people — be they Japanese Americans or others — never forget what the redress movement was about and what an enormous battle it was for us to achieve vindication. The road to redress was unpaved and rocky, a ten-year quest full of obstacles and disappointments. Yet, we hung on because we believed in justice. And justice did finally prevail.

Epilogue

From my vantage point, I continue to marvel at Sox's unconditional commitment to her community, and by extension, her country. Sox puts her heart and soul into helping total strangers because she cares about the fundamental American values of justice, fairness, and equality. Add to that her belief in perseverance and limitless compassion. Her life and her life's work truly reflect those ideals.

Touching Lives in the Heartland

I must relate a story about Sox's visit to the state of Indiana in 1995, where I lived for several years. Sox gave the keynote address at the opening reception of the Smithsonian Institution's traveling exhibit, "A More Perfect Union: Japanese Americans and the United States Constitution," which premiered at the Tippecanoe County Public Library in Lafayette, Indiana. She addressed a standing-room-only crowd that included local and state political dignitaries, educators, media, and area residents. You could have heard a pin drop during her speech. By the time she finished her talk, there was not a dry eye in sight. For most, it was the first time they had ever heard about the internment camps.

Sox expressed a strong desire to speak with schoolchildren during her stay. Ms. Mary Lee Webeck, an innovative teacher who has implemented studies of the internment in her curriculum, invited her to speak at a rural elementary and middle school in Monticello, Indiana. Ms. Webeck had read about Sox in Teaching Tolerance magazine, a free publication produced by the Southern Poverty Law Center in Alabama and distributed to educators across the country. She had her class read about Sox. The students were thrilled that someone "famous" was coming to speak, a rarity in a town like Monticello.

The teacher had warned Sox that Monticello has a long established and active Ku Klux Klan presence and that some students are openly and proudly KKK members. Do not be dismayed if some students seem uninterested, Ms. Webeck said to Sox. Undeterred, Sox spoke to an attentive and excited group of three hundred sixth- and seventh-graders about her life behind barbed wire. After her talk, Sox fielded dozens of questions from students and teachers alike. When she finished, a group of students surged toward her, thanking her for coming to speak and wanting to know more about her life. One student quietly asked Sox if he could give her a hug because he was very moved by what she had to say.

Sox visited with one of the sixth-grade classes, where eager and curious students asked more questions. One student, a blond-haired, blue-eyed boy, asked Sox if she thought she was a "hero." Taken aback, Sox said, "Me? A hero? No way! Why do you ask that?" The boy replied, "Because I think you're one." Sox was shocked. She asked, "Why would you think that?" "Because you're trying to educate people about what happened," he replied. It speaks volumes that a sixth-grader from a small, rural town in Indiana would make the association that a hero could indeed be a seventy-eight-year-old Japanese American grandmother from California.

Those of us who care deeply about Sox sometimes worry that she gives too much of herself to others. Maybe she should learn to just say "no" to the constant demands on her time and energy. It's difficult to keep up with her hectic schedule: She is usually running from one board meeting to another, giving talks at schools, or volunteering for yet another fundraiser. While a recent knee replacement operation has slowed her down physically, she continues to give selflessly and without hesitation.

In our hearts, we all know Sox wouldn't have it any other way. That is simply her nature. So I, like others, try to quash the protective feelings we have for her by remembering that she is happiest when she is doing things for others. Her parents would be very proud indeed.

APPENDIX

The U.S. Justice Department effort to identify, locate and ultimately compensate individuals who were interned during WWII
was one of the most daunting tasks I had been involved with in
over twenty years of government service. The U.S. Congress had
high expectations that the Department would administer this
program differently than most other Federal programs.
Executing the program would require unprecedented partner-
ship with the Japanese American community. During my four
years as Administrator, there were many individuals who gave
significant effort above and beyond what was expected to make
this program the success. Without a doubt, Sox is one of the first
persons to come to mind as one of those individuals who worked
hard and tirelessly for the Redress program.

From the very first day of the program, her commitment and
strong work ethic were evident. She often worked into the night
and on weekends. She was constantly engaged in the cause,
focused on the end game, and very interested in learning the
details about on our next visit. No sooner had we expanded our
regulations to include another group of individuals who were
overlooked, when Sox would present another compelling case for
redress. She was one of the reasons I believe we left no stone
unturned.

The style in which she conducted her business with the
Department was equally as impressive as her commitment to the
program. She is a motivator who makes everyone around her *want*

to help. I remember receiving a phone call from her on the weekend. It was regarding a Peruvian individual whom Sox believed should be eligible for redress. She made a compelling case for redress. It is undeniable that the program — and ultimately many Japanese Americans—benefited from her judgment, which is one of the reasons she is so special to all of us at the department. When I think of redress, I think of Sox. She really made a difference.

ROBERT K. BRATT
FORMER ADMINISTRATOR
OFFICE OF REDRESS ADMINISTRATION
FEBRUARY 2003

Many know Sox as a redress activist, an outspoken advocate for seniors, educator of the Japanese American camp experience, and tireless volunteer in the San Francisco Japanese American community. For inspiring a community, she is recognized as a role model. For her dedication to social justice, she is a woman warrior. For her volunteer leadership and service to the community, she is the referred to as the "godmother" of Japantown. Sox is, indeed, all of that and much more. She is a friend. She cares very deeply about her family, friends and community. Her love for others and commitment to making this a better place is heard through her voice in conversations, interviews, speeches, and now, in this book. Those who have heard Sox speak at forums or rallies know that she concluded each speech with words of appreciation and "I love you all!" Sox, it's our turn. On behalf of all those whose lives you've touched, I say, "Thank you, and we love you!"

CAROLE HAYASHINO
FORMER NATIONAL ASSOCIATE DIRECTOR
JAPANESE AMERICAN CITIZENS LEAGUE
JULY 2003

It is easy to recognize Sox Kitashima-short stature, the pure white hair framing a dark-complexion and a pixie-ish, youthful face. Images of a grandmother, a "little old lady," sweet and kind come to mind. But the external appearance is misleading because Sox Kitashima is much, much more than what she seems to be.

I first met her during the heady days of the Redress Movement. Sox was a tireless worker for Redress and Reparations, organizing letter writing campaigns, calling on our leaders to support the Redress bill, lobbying congress, pushing everyone she knew (and those she didn't know to fight for the bill. She was omnipresent — at every meeting, every rally, every assemblage where Redress was a topic. Though she is many years older than I, she made me feel old.

Her work for Redress was legendary, but she never stopped to rest after the Redress bill was signed into law. She continued her activism, searching for eligible recipients and insisting that they apply for Redress, persuading, cajoling, even demanding that Japanese Americans obtain the full measure of their lost political birthright. Somewhere down the path of that inspired journey, she became a leader lending a strong voice not only t to the Japanese American community but to all communities that were suffering the indignities of discrimination. She became not just a "Japanese American" civil rights activist but also an "American" spokesperson for justice. Along the way, she inspired everyone she met with her strength, courage and steely focus.

But her political efforts reveal only a part of a complete personality. She treated friends as family and strangers as friends, offering small and large acts of generosity. When I moved into the house I bought, this retiree on Social Security sent me $100 as a housewarming gift. When we moved into a new law office, she and her friend, Katherine Nunotani, volunteered to make *sushi* for our office opening. Her kindness was an integral part of her compassion for others.

That kindness and generosity, however, should not be taken for weakness as Sox can be disarmingly direct, challenging you to do more, try harder and be better not with an ingratiating style but by simply telling you what you should do. I learned this through the many events we both attended and during our several meals together when we would talk and argue about politics, community, and family. Her appetite for new ideas, stimulating conversation, and good food, I learned, was enormous.

So to describe Sox in a simple phrase or even a paragraph is impossible as she embraces and embodies the fullness of human emotions. She can begin crying in a nanosecond about anything that touches her heart; she can also read you the riot act if she feels you are not doing what you should to advance social justice. But if I had to describe her in a phrase, I think of her as the purest heart I ever met. And for that alone, despite her other wonderful qualities, I think of her as my hero.

Dale Minami
Attorney and Lead Counsel for
Fred Korematsu in *Korematsu v. U.S.* (1983)
January 2003

Honors & Awards

In light of her many significant contributions to the Japanese American community and public at large, Sox has received numerous local, state, and national awards.

In 1993, Sox received a national award from the U.S. Department of Justice for Outstanding Public Service. A surprise party was held in Sox's honor on January 7, 1993, at the Miyako Hotel in San Francisco's Japantown. Sox was stunned when she entered the ballroom of the hotel to the cheers of everyone in attendance. Thinking she was going to a political fundraiser, she was at first confused, then embarrassed, when she realized that hundreds of people were there to honor her. A master at event planning and paying attention to detail, Carole Hayashino, former national associate director of the JACL and the event coordinator, had provided guests and Sox with little packets of tissue because Sox is fondly known for crying rivers of tears when she becomes emotional.

The plaque was presented to Sox by former ORA Administrator Robert (Bob) K. Bratt, and his deputy Paul Suddes, on behalf of the U.S. Attorney General, William Barr, and John Dunne, Assistant Attorney General. It read:

"In recognition and appreciation of the meritorious acts and service which have materially contributed to the attainment of the highest standards of law enforcement and justice in the United States of America."

Paul Suddes noted that the award was backdated to "a very important date:" February 19, 1992, the golden anniversary of Executive Order 9066.

Sox's family also played an important part in the evening's festivities. Her son and grandson had a chance to speak publicly about their very public mother and grandmother. In an emotional tribute, Sox's son Alan spoke about being known around Japantown as "Sox's son."

"Mom," he said, "I know I don't have to tell you how proud I am of you. But tonight, in front of all these people, I want to say how very proud I am. . . I'd like to quote John F. Kennedy, in his inaugural address in which he said, 'Ask not what your country can do for you, ask what you can do for your country.' What my mom has done for her country was to help make it aware of the grave injustice to Japanese Americans during World War II. She helped to open the public's eyes to help right a wrong. Mom, thank you for your hard work and your dedication. My only regret is that my dad is not here to share this moment with us. I know his spirit's here."

Alan was followed by his son Aaron, age ten: "Dear grandma, I love you very much. I'm happy that you are getting all these nice awards. Keep working hard to help other people. I'm proud to be your grandson."

Of that night, Sox says in retrospect, "It took me a long time to come back down to earth."

Local, State and National Recognition

ALUMNAE RESOURCES, WAVE (WOMEN OF ACHIEVEMENT, VISION AND EXCELLENCE) AWARD

ASIAN AMERICAN JAZZ FESTIVAL

ASIAN PACIFIC AMERICAN DEMOCRATIC CLUB, "LIVING TREASURE" AWARD

CITY AND COUNTY OF SAN FRANCISCO

COMMISSION ON THE STATUS OF WOMEN, CITY OF SAN FRANCISCO

THE FREEDOM FORUM, "FREE SPIRIT" AWARD

JAPANESE AMERICAN CITIZENS LEAGUE

JAPANESE CULTURAL AND COMMUNITY CENTER OF NORTHERN CALIFORNIA

KRON-TV, SAN FRANCISCO, "FOR THOSE WHO CARE" AWARD

KQED-TV, SAN FRANCISCO

KIMOCHI, INC.

NATIONAL COALITION FOR REDRESS AND REPARATIONS

PACIFIC ASIAN AMERICAN WOMAN BAY AREA COALITION, WOMAN WARRIOR AWARD

SAN FRANCISCO BOARD OF SUPERVISORS

SAN FRANCISCO REDEVELOPMENT AGENCY'S GENE SUTTLE PLAZA STREETSCAPE IMPROVEMENT PROJECT

SAN FRANCISCO STATE UNIVERSITY'S GARDEN OF REMEMBRANCE

STATE OF CALIFORNIA, LEGISLATIVE ASSEMBLY

STATE OF HAWAI`I, HOUSE OF REPRESENTATIVES

UNITY NEWSPAPER

Profiled in *Us and Them* ("The Shadow of Hate," a free teaching kit on intolerance in America, produced by the Southern Poverty Law Center)

Profiled in *Grandmother Book* by Patricia Burstein and Jessica Burstein, St. Martin's Press, 2000

Profiled in *The American Dream: Stories from the Heart of Our Nation* by Dan Rather, HarperCollins Publishers Inc., New York, 2001

Profiled in *The Columbia Documentary History of the Asian American Experience*, Franklin Odo, ed. Columbia University Press, New York, 2002.

Endnotes

[1] Ronald Takaki, *A Different Mirror, A History of Multicultural America*, (Boston: Little, Brown and Co., 1993), 248. Many Japanese immigrant men sent for their future brides in Japan via proxy. Photographs would be exchanged between the prospective bride and groom with a go-between usually negotiating with the two families.

[2] Him Mark Lai, Genny Lim, and Judy Yung, *Island: Poetry and History of Chinese Immigrants on Angel Island, 1910-1940,* (Seattle: University of Washington Press, 1980), 13. Prior to 1910, immigration inspectors detained Chinese and other Asian immigrants in a two-story shed at the Pacific Mail Steamship Company wharf. Hundreds of immigrants were often confined to this shed. Judy Yung, *Chinese Women of America, A Pictorial History*, (Seattle: University of Washington Press, 1986), 42. After 1910, Asian immigrants were processed through an immigration station located in San Francisco Bay called Angel Island — often referred to as the Ellis Island of the West. They were subjected to rigorous interrogation and physical examinations, a process which could last anywhere from two weeks to two years, and lived in "prison-like barracks."

[3] Frank F. Chuman, *The Bamboo People: The Law and Japanese Americans,* (Chicago: Japanese American Research Project, Japanese American Citizens League, 1976), 70–71. In the case of *Ozawa vs. U.S.* (1922), the United States Supreme Court ruled that Japanese aliens (and, by extension, other Asians) were ineligible for naturalization and United States citizenship because they were neither "free white persons" nor persons of "African nativity."

Naturalization privileges were denied to Japanese aliens until 1952. The Alien Land Laws of 1913 and 1920 in California, which were similar to laws adopted in other states, prohibited aliens from owning land. Aliens were only allowed to lease land for a period of three years. Some Issei circumvented the laws by placing land in the names of their children, who were American citizens. Further restrictions, however, were later adopted.

[4] A popular and colorful annual festival in which the souls of dead ancestors are said to temporarily return home, and the living pay respect to their souls and spirits.

[5] Traditional rhythmic, repetitive dances; each movement has significance and is meant to soothe the spirits of the dead.

[6] Michi Weglyn, *Years of Infamy*, (New York: William Morrow, 1976), 76. "Repression was applied, one small step at a time. First came the roundup of suspect enemy aliens, the freezing of bank accounts, the seizure of contraband, the drastic limitation on travel, curfew, and other restrictive measures of increasing severity."

[7] Japanese Americans forcibly removed from the West Coast prior to their detention and internment in American concentration camps were referred to as "evacuees" by government officials.

[8] Sandra C. Taylor, *Jewel of the Desert: Japanese American Internment at Topaz,* (Berkeley: University of California Press, 1993), 38. In 1940, about thirteen hundred Japanese Americans resided in the Mount Eden and Washington townships. Even though less than twenty-five percent of the Japanese American farmers owned land, they had invested over a million dollars in their nurseries, farms, and homes.

[9] E.g., Chuman, *The Bamboo People: The Law and Japanese Americans*, 8–11, 40–41, 48. America's history of racial discrimination against Asians had its origins in the mid-1800s when the immigration of Chinese to America began. For example, The Chinese Exclusion Act of 1882, passed by Congress, was intended to strip the Chinese of all legal rights and to prevent the establishment of a permanent Chinese population in the United States. This was the first time a group of people were excluded on the basis of race. The Chinese were deemed "aliens" ineligible for

U.S. citizenship. Nearly all immigration of Chinese to America was prohibited.

The Japanese immigrants, who succeeded the Chinese to this country, also became targets of prejudice and discrimination and faced similar barriers in their attempts to make America home. The Asian Exclusion Act of 1924 barred all Japanese immigrants from permanent residence in the United States. Alien Land Laws in California effectively prohibited Japanese from owning land. Anti-miscegenation laws prohibited them from marrying outside of their race. Hundreds of discriminatory and restrictive laws were enacted against the Chinese and Japanese.

Allan R. Bosworth, *America's Concentration Camps*, (New York: W.W. Norton, 1967), 38–40. Organizations such as the Native Sons and Daughters of the Golden West, the Oriental Exclusion League, labor unions, agricultural groups, the California Joint Immigration Committee, various Japanese Exclusion Leagues, politicians, and many newspapers and columnists continually maligned the Japanese and Chinese as a growing and threatening "yellow peril." Pressure groups called for the expulsion of Japanese from America. Propaganda and sensationalistic journalism flourished and fed, and fed upon, the growing tide of resentment toward Asians in America.

[10] "Detention camps" are used interchangeably with "internment camps" and "concentration camps." U.S. Government officials euphemistically referred to these guarded compounds as "relocation centers" and "assembly centers."

[11] National Japanese American Historical Society (NJAHS), *Americans of Japanese Ancestry and the United States Constitution: 1787–1987*, (San Francisco: National Japanese American Historical Society, 1987), 40. The term "internees" refers to Japanese Americans incarcerated and confined in the temporary and permanent camps.

[12] Weglyn, *Years of Infamy*, 42; NJAHS, *Americans of Japanese Ancestry and the United States Constitution: 1787–1987*, 26. At the time of the internment, the average age of the Issei was about sixty; for the Nisei, it was eighteen. There were over fifteen thousand children under ten years of age in the camps, and another two thousand children under the age of five.

About two thousand people over the age of sixty-five were sent to the camps, as were one thousand seriously handicapped or bedridden individuals.

[13] Taylor, *Jewel of the Desert*, 69. Visits by outsiders were limited to two hours in the morning and three hours in the afternoon. Barred from entering the grounds, living quarters, or mess hall, visitors were required to have a pass and their parcels inspected.

[14] Goro Suzuki later became a Hollywood actor. His stage name was Jack Soo. He landed a regular role in the TV series "Barney Miller."

[15] Other camps included Gila River and Poston, Arizona; Granada, Colorado; Heart Mountain, Wyoming; Jerome and Rohwer, Arkansas; Minidoka, Idaho; and Manzanar and Tule Lake, California.

[16] Taylor, *Jewel of the Desert*, 90. The first sizable group of internees entered Topaz on September 17, 1942, the last group on October 11, 1942. Internees arrived at the rate of five hundred a day.

[17] Taylor, *Jewel of the Desert*, 97.

[18] Ibid., 72-74, 135. A block manager created and implemented rules by which the internees lived. Managers served as liaisons between the two hundred and fifty to three hundred block residents and the Caucasian administrators. Appointed by the administrators, managers, it should be noted, often became natural scapegoats when people's needs were not met.

[19] Ibid., 113. Beginning in October 1942, Utah farmers recruited young men and women from the camp to help in the fields as seasonal laborers. Due to the labor shortage produced by the war, it became increasingly popular for farmers in the surrounding areas to come to the camp seeking laborers.

[20] Ibid., 93-96. The Topaz internment camp eventually consisted of four hundred and eight buildings. Over time, a community auditorium, gymnasium, canteens, schools, libraries, churches, a post office, fire station, and cemetery — which went unused — were constructed. The one hundred and forty-four people who eventually died at Topaz were cremated and their ashes returned to the Northern California area after the war.

[21] Ibid., 114-115. Wages for internees ranged from sixteen to twenty-one dollars a month and were purposely kept low so that Japanese Americans would not earn more than a U.S. Army private.

While Army wages increased over the course of the war, however, internees' wages were kept constant. By comparison, wages in the outside world were manyfold higher. Teachers, for example, could earn one hundred and fifty to two hundred dollars a month.

[22] Ibid., 96. The WRA set the internees' food allowance at forty-five cents a day per person, a nickel lower than the military allowance.

[23] Ibid., 227. "Some administrators were sympathetic to the Nikkei's [Japanese Americans] plight, and a few were overtly hostile; most were simply neutral."

[24] NJAHS, *Americans of Japanese Ancestry and the United States Constitution: 1787–1987*, 54.

[25] Taylor, *Jewel of the Desert*, 141. Security in the camps fell under the control of the military. Combat veterans and "less capable men who were clearly trigger-happy" were assigned to Topaz. The Wakasa shooting "made the guards more careful but not necessarily less determined to prevent 'escapes' of the people they identified as the enemy."

[26] Ibid., 113. Although ambiguous at best, the WRA's leave policy encouraged resettlement of the Japanese American population away from the West Coast.

[27] Weglyn, *Years of Infamy*, 139. "One of the basic underlying objectives of the registration [questionnaire] had been to speed up, on a mass basis, the clearing of loyal adults for resettlement."

[28] Taylor, *Jewel of the Desert*, 153. About one thousand, four hundred and forty-seven internees left Topaz for Tule Lake (one thousand and sixty-two Nisei and three hundred and eighty-five Issei).

[29] NJAHS, *Americans of Japanese Ancestry and the United States Constitution: 1787–1987*, 59, 67–68; Takaki, *A Different Mirror, A History of Multicultural America*, 383–84.

[30] Taylor, *Jewel of the Desert*, 185. WRA policy: Twenty-five dollars to each internee as a resettlement grant, fifty dollars for a family.

[31] Weglyn, Years of Infamy, 77. "A postwar survey was to reveal that eighty percent of goods privately stored were 'rifled, stolen or sold during absence.'"

[32] Until 1952, Japanese and other Asian immigrants were effectively barred from becoming naturalized U.S. citizens. With the passage of the Immigration and Nationality Act of 1952, more commonly known as the McCarran-Walter Act, Japanese immigrants were finally allowed naturalization.

[33] Founded in 1929, the Japanese American Citizens League (JACL) is the nation's oldest and largest Asian American civil rights organization; the National Coalition for Redress and Reparations (NCRR) was founded in 1980 to uphold the constitutional, civil, and human rights of Japanese Americans, Asian/Pacific Islanders, and all Americans; the National Council for Japanese American Redress (NCJAR) sought to address redress directly through the courts by filing a multibillion class action suit on behalf of Japanese Americans in 1983.

[34] John Tateishi, "The Japanese American Citizens League and the Struggle for Redress." In Roger Daniels, Sandra C. Taylor, and Harry H.L. Kitano, eds. *Japanese Americans From Relocation to Redress*, (Salt Lake City: University of Utah Press, 1986), 193-194.

[35] They included: Joan Z. Bernstein, chair of the Commission and former general counsel of the U.S. Department of Health and Human Services; Congressman Daniel E. Lungren of Long Beach, California, vice chair; former U.S. Sen. Edward W. Brooke; Rev. Robert F. Drinan, president of Americans for Democratic Action and a former U.S. congressman; Dr. Arthur S. Flemming, chair of the U.S. Commission on Civil Rights; the Hon. Arthur J. Goldberg, a former Supreme Court justice and former ambassador to the United Nations; Father Ishmael V. Gromoff, a former Aleutian internee; former U.S. Sen. Hugh B. Mitchell; and Judge William M. Marutani, the only Japanese American on the commission. Angus Macbeth served as special counsel.

[36] These individuals included Nellie Takeda, Hatsy Yasukochi, John Yasumoto, Lucy Hamai, Momo Hatamiya, Yoshitomo Fukushima, and my sister-in-law Yo Kitashima.

[37] Members included Marlene Tonai, Naomi Kubota, John Ota, Laurie Ozoni, Don Misumi.

[38] Leslie T. Hatamiya, *Righting a Wrong: Japanese Americans and the Passage of the Civil Liberties Act of 1988,* (Stanford: Stanford University Press, 1993), 166-171.

[39] Ibid., 173-177.

[40] Ibid., 57.

[41] Ibid.

[42] Eric Saul, curator of the National Japanese American Historical Society, was instrumental in coordinating the 442nd RCT's participation.

[43] Hatamiya, *Righting a Wrong,* 58.

[44] Ibid.

[45] Ibid., 120-121. The inclusion of restitution for Aleutian Islanders who were mistreated by the U.S. government during World War II was a separate and unrelated issue that the House of Representatives initially wanted addressed in a separate bill. However, the two issues were kept together in the Senate; Republican Sen. Ted Stevens of Alaska was a ranking and key minority member of the subcommittee overseeing the Japanese American redress bill. Hatamiya writes, "In essence, the combination of the two issues of redress in the Civil Liberties Act of 1988 proved to be a successful marriage of political convenience."

[46] Ibid., 151-152. Framing the redress issue around ideology and principle, *i.e.*, a constitutional issue as opposed to a racial issue, and one based on equal opportunity as a fundamental American value guaranteed by the Constitution, successfully appealed to President Reagan and other conservatives.

[47] Ibid., 162-163. Kazuo (Kaz) Masuda was a member of the Japanese American 442nd RCT who died in combat. Despite having received the Distinguished Service Cross, the community of Santa Ana, California, where he was to be laid to rest, opposed his burial in the local cemetery. In an attempt to mitigate the community's opposition, Ronald Reagan, then a popular actor, Gen. "Vinegar Joe" Stillwell, and other local personalities attended a ceremony to posthumously award Masuda's family the Distinguished Service Cross in 1945.

Ironically, the medal was presented to Kazuo's sister, who was an American citizen, and not to his Issei mother, who was an alien. In 1987, New Jersey Gov. Thomas Kean, who personally lobbied President Reagan to support the redress bill, reminded him of the story of Kaz Masuda.

[48] The Japanese Cultural and Community Center of Northern California (JCCCNC) serves the evolving needs of the Japanese American community through its programs, services and facilities.

[49] Kimochi, Inc. is a San Francisco-based, multi-service organization for Japanese American seniors. Refer to Chapter XV.

[50] Restitution for Aleutians was covered under a separate category.

[51] Hatamiya, *Righting a Wrong,* 181.

[52] Members of this contingent included non-NCRR members as well. Those who participated were Trisha Murakawa (JACL), Miya Iwataki (NCRR-Los Angeles), Sue Tokushige (Nihonmachi Outreach Committee of San Jose, an organization dedicated to educating the public about the forced evacuation and incarceration of Japanese Americans during World War II), Rudy Tokiwa (442nd veteran), Dorothy and Ted Kojima (NCRR-Los Angeles), UC Berkeley student and NCRR member Brent Mori, as well as San Francisco-NCRR members Fred and Kathryn Korematsu, Katherine Nunotani, and John Ota.

[53] Initial government estimates found that former internees were dying at a rate of two hundred a month.

[54] The paper crane became a symbol of peace in Japan after World War II. An eleven-year-old Japanese schoolgirl named Sadako Sasaki developed leukemia after being exposed to radiation from the atomic bombs. She was told that if she folded one thousand paper cranes, her wish to live would be granted. Sadako began folding, but died after completing just six hundred and forty-four cranes. As a tribute to her and her wish for peace around the world, Sadako's schoolmates finished folding the rest of the cranes and helped erect a monument in her memory in Hiroshima. Today, people around the world, particularly schoolchildren, send paper cranes to Sadako's memorial to symbolize their hope for world peace.

[55] Examples of other entitlement, or mandatory domestic spending programs, include Social Security, Medicare, welfare, military and civil service pensions, and food stamps.

[56] AsianImprov Records, Oakland, California. Record number AIR0007; September, 1989.

[57] A Japanese doll with missing eyes. It is customary to make a wish and fill in one eye. When the wish is fulfilled, the other eye is drawn in to make the doll complete.

[58] Sen. Spark Matsunaga (D-Hawai`i) died on April 15, 1990, before presentation of the first redress payments. Regarded as one of the hardest-working and most popular senators, Matsunaga was a decorated World War II veteran who rose through the ranks of the Senate to become Chief Deputy Majority Whip. He is credited with singlehandedly lobbying every one of his colleagues to support redress legislation. The results were extraordinary, as seventy-five senators eventually signed on to S. 1009 (Civil Liberties Act of 1988). After his death, Rep. Daniel Akaka (D- Hawai` i), also a firm supporter of redress, succeeded Senator Matsunaga.

[59] Established in 1975, Nihonmachi Legal Outreach (NLO), now called Asian Pacific Islander Legal Outreach, is a nonprofit social justice law firm serving the San Francisco Bay Area Asian American and Pacific Islander communities.

[60] The National Japanese American Historical Society (NJAHS), founded in 1980, is a nonprofit membership supported organization dedicated to the preservation, promotion and dissemination of materials relating to the history and culture of Japanese Americans.

[61] The Japanese American National Library is a community library located in San Francisco's Japantown that collects and preserves books and documents on Japanese Americans.

[62] Hatamiya, *Righting a Wrong*, 188.

[63] Weglyn, *Years of Infamy*, 56-57, 60, 64. Due to U.S. pressure on its allied countries to preserve security in the Western Hemisphere, "enemy aliens," specifically those of Japanese ancestry, were rounded up and

detained or evacuated in Canada, Mexico, Central America, and other countries. The option of deporting such "potentially dangerous" individuals to the United States was extended by our government and readily agreed to by the Peruvian government, which was becoming increasingly hostile toward its Japanese-Peruvian citizens. At war's end, the Peruvian government refused these citizens reentry into Peru. Incredulously, the United States government attempted to deport Japanese-Peruvians to Japan, claming they had entered the United States "illegally."

[64] Formed in 1992, the Japanese Peruvian Oral History Project documents the experiences of Japanese Latin Americans.

[65] Asian Law Alliance is a community law office that provides individual legal assistance, community legal education, and community advocacy for the Asian Pacific Islander community of Santa Clara County, California.

[66] Community people in attendance included Roz Enomoto and San Mateo JACL members, Wally and Katherine Nunotani, Jim and Mary Kajiwara, Teru Kanba, J.K. Yamamoto, Fred and Kathryn Korematsu, Lillian Kiyota, Chiyeko Yukawa, and Chiz and Ernie Iiyama.

[67] Night Riders are synonymous with the Ku Klux Klan, a white supremacist hate group.

[68] Founded in 1995, the Asian American Arts Foundation is currently inactive.

[69] The Asian Law Caucus promotes, advances, and represents the legal and civil rights of Asian Pacific Islander communities throughout Northern California.